Ashes of the Phoenix

A COLLECTION OF HEALING POEMS

MICHOL MAE

EDITED BY JEN VALENTINO

EDITED BY BRANDI LOVEDAY-CHESLEY

EDITED BY ANGELA SWOVELAND

FOREWORD BY LAURA DIFRANCO

ILLUSTRATED BY MICHOL MAE

Contents

Disclaimer

The information presented in this book is based on the author's experience and opinions and does not constitute any health or medical advice. While the author hopes this content will help you in your journey toward healing, the content of this book is informational and voluntary and is not intended to diagnose, treat, cure, or prevent any condition or disease.

Please seek advice from your healthcare provider for your personal health concerns.

At the time of release, the following resources are available:

The 988 Lifeline provides 24/7, accessible, and confidential support for people in distress, prevention and crisis resources for you or your loved ones, and best practices for professionals in the United States.

Help and support are available right now in the UK if you need it for difficult feelings. Text "SHOUT" to 85258 or call 116 123.

Dedication

This book is dedicated to everyone who has ever crossed my path or joined me for a while on my journey. Everyone who touches our lives shapes our lives.

Also, to my sister Sandra for advocating for me to pursue writing since we were in High School.

This book would not have been possible without my soul sister Angie. Without her infectious enthusiasm for my upcoming fiction, I may never have meaningfully returned to writing.

It takes confidence to write a book and release it to the world. Thank you to my soul sister Brandi, an amazing writer herself, for the encouragement and persistence that helped give me more confidence.

The release of this book faltered for a few years before Laura Di Franco came into my life. Being accepted as co-author in 100 Poems & Possibilities for Healing opened the door to more possibilities. Becoming a best-selling author helped stop my self-sabotage. Her wise words also helped me challenge my imposter syndrome more readily.

Thank you to my editor, Jen Valentino, I'm so glad our paths crossed. Your encouragement has kept me moving forward and given me much needed structure and deadlines, which were delivered with love and spirit.

Preface

I've been writing poetry since I was a child. I started writing in middle school when someone gave me a Maya Angelo notebook to write my thoughts in. I read her poems and found further inspiration. Writing was a way for me to process and heal my emotions and deal with some very tumultuous and traumatic life-altering events.

In this book, you hold all the poetry I have written from those days until as recently as this book went to the editor. Each chapter has a theme arranged in chronological order. In this way, you can not only experience my poetry, but I invite you to experience pieces of my life, history, healing, and journey.

It was challenging in some cases to keep the poetry in its original state, having grown and learned so much over the years. Yet, I found value in its elementary form watching the growth myself as I put the pages together. I hope you will find value as well.

Writing can be very healing, and I was fortunate enough to have someone suggest that I write to process my feelings at a noticeably early age. This is the reason I have included space for you to write at the end of each chapter. I hope that if the pages in this book resonate with you, one of the takeaways is a sense that you are not alone. My intention is, by the end, that you will feel the genuine possibility of healing. I hope this leads you to step forward, embrace yourself, and move toward your dreams.

Throughout this book, you will see a Haiku at the start of each chapter. A Haiku is written by syllable count in three lines. Traditional Japanese Haiku are said to be about nature. Non-conventional Haiku can be written about any subject. To write a Haiku you pick your topic and follow the 5/7/5 syllable rule. Five syllables for the first line, seven syllables for the second line, and five syllables for the last line. Here are three Haikus from my written works.

~

Cold wind burnt my face,
The bitter wind is not bad,
I learned from it, warmth.

Grief waves will hit you,
But I promise they will ebb,
Lean in, breathe again.

Perfect Poetry,
precious possibilities,
on paper perfect.

Healing words of soul,
In music and written form,
Save my life once more.

Foreword

BY LAURA DI FRANCO, SPOKEN WORD POET, AND CEO OF
BRAVE HEALER PRODUCTIONS

Some think about poetry and say, "It's never been my thing." When I hear
that, I literally have to cover my mouth to stop myself from asking, "What's
wrong with you!? You mean love isn't your thing? You mean the attempts to
put the feeling of the full moon or stars, or any of life's hardest moments or
biggest joys on paper to heal the world isn't for you?"

From Michol's first invitation into her private world and whole-life
collection of healing poems, you'll do more than read poetry, you'll feel
these things. And what a gift it is to have a safe place to do that, to give your-
self permission to feel everything, and then allow yourself the deep explo-
ration into your own heart and soul that her poems urge.

In *Ashes of the Phoenix* we can taste our own feathers burning, but without
fear, dive into the fire of Michol's beautiful, kind, generous, sometimes sad,
and most always brilliant words. A poet, writer, and performer, Michol's
collection is for the New Earth, a path to transformation, a call to action for
our world's healers to become a stronger community. She does this with

respect and takes responsibility for using her vulnerability as her strength, one mark of a true warrior.

I hope you let yourself be uncomfortable on some pages and experience the bliss contained in others. Let yourself be moved. Pause and breathe. Notice what's in you to feel. Take her up on the spaces she includes for your soul to speak your own words. These are some of the ways Michol is changing the world in this book. It's way more than poetry.

I'm so completely honored that she invited me to add a few of my words to this book—this gift—and I am thoroughly excited because I know what treasures of healing are waiting here for you.

With warrior love,

Laura

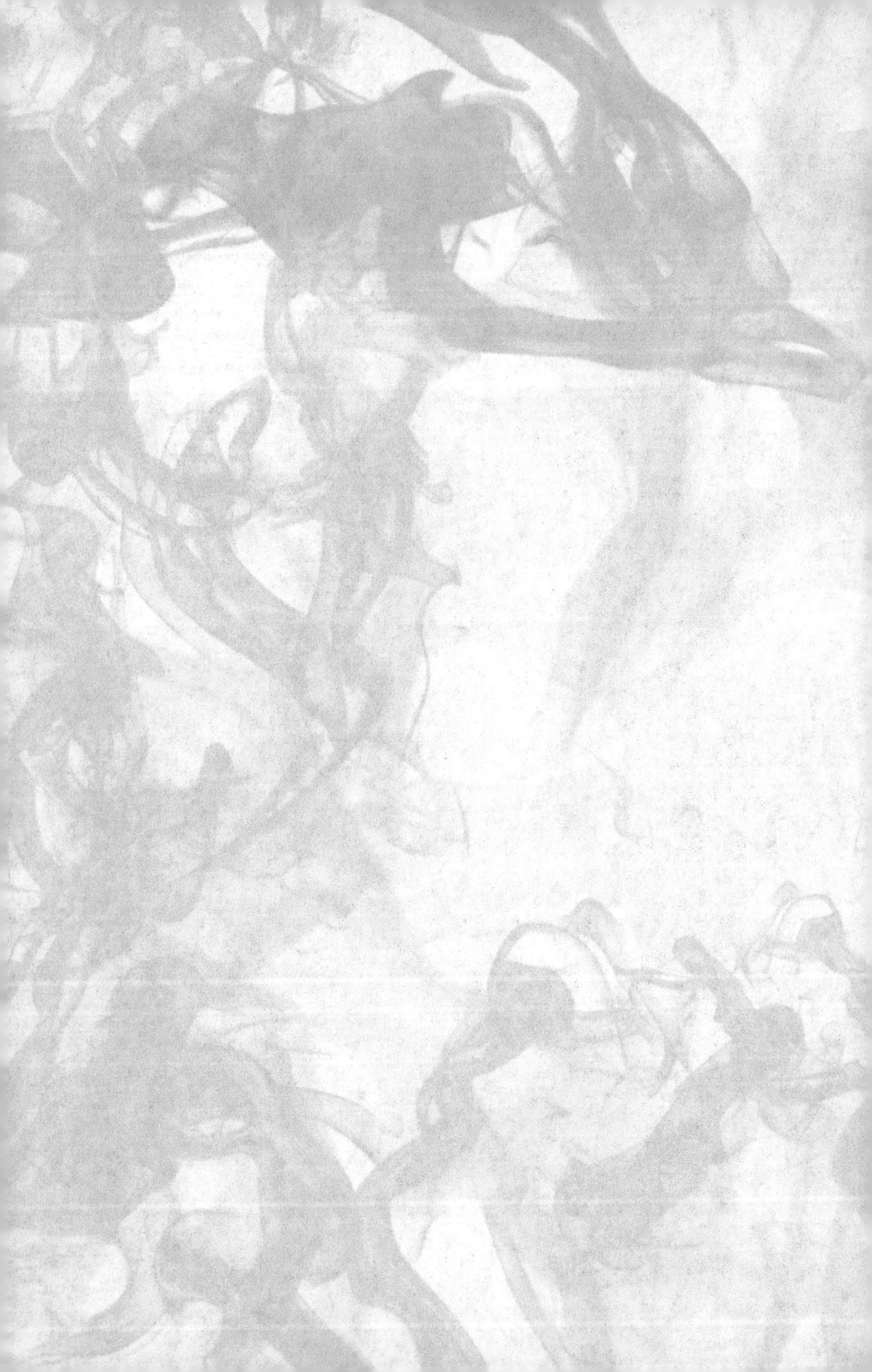

Land of Misfit Poems

Though I was young then,
My bad experiences,
Taught hard life lessons.

~

This chapter and the chapters beyond this point are organized from the earliest written works to the most current. This chapter holds poems that didn't fit neatly in the other chapter categories. The first poem, *Seriously Misunderstood*, was written when I was a teenager and was accepted into a poetry anthology that encouraged me further on my path toward writing. A few poems throughout these chapters have been granted the editor's choice award by the anthology publisher at that time. I hope that when you read the poetry in this chapter, you remember you are not alone. My intention, when I decided to release this book, was to offer comfort and encouragement. You will see first-hand there were times I wasn't sure I'd survive, but I did. And if you've ever felt that way, I want you to know that you can too. It was important to me that this book be a safe space, providing hope and proof that although we struggle, we can come out the other side. You have survived 100 percent of the things life has thrown at you. Now, it is time for you to thrive.

SERIOUSLY MISUNDERSTOOD

*** As previously published in *By the Light of the Moon* by The Poetry Guild

She dances, she sings, and loves everything.

She's peaceful and kind but a little bit shy.

Deep inside, she feels so kind,

But it doesn't always show on the outside.

People must learn beauty comes from within,

And the truth is as cold as the coldest wind.

Being different is not a sin,

But somehow, shows a gift within.

Many are kind, but more are cruel,

And only seem to want the biggest jewel.

Look inside your heart and think really hard,

What makes us all apart?

We are not all the same, none of us are,

Some of us just have a colder heart.

What could make someone so cruel?

Is it someone you know, or is it you?

Is it the lack of freedom that some of us have,

Or was it a wrong choice that made you sad?
No one is completely different, no one is the same,

Yet some treat others as if they live in another day,

Everyone's a judge, and that's just what they do,

And now I find no one really knows the truth,

Because they never took the time to know you for you.

STAR IN THE SKY

I am a star in the sky, untouchable,

If you try to touch me, your hand will burn and crumble.

I am a star in the sky out of reach,

So that hurt and pain can never touch me.

I am a star in the sky, untouchable,

You could try to hold me but are unable.

I am a star in the sky far from the Earth,

Where the people are so cold and filled with hurt.

I am a star in the sky beyond the sea,

So, you will never have the chance to reach me.

I am a star in the sky you can see,

But I will not let anyone else hurt me.

I AM THE GIRL

I am the girl in the trees mysterious,

The one who everyone comes, to smile at least once,

I am the girl who plays and has fun,

And the girl who is capable of a great love who is loved.

I am the girl whose friends turn to, to make them smile,

The girl who's witty and quirky and likes to laugh a while,

I am the girl who gets sad only once in a while,

And no one can see; she keeps it hidden in guile.

I am a girl who learned from mistakes in the past,

I am the girl who survived by learning to just laugh.

WHY

The river runs wild, through huge forest trees.

Like a girl in love, she is never at ease.

Broken hearts, that never mend,

Remind her of the river bend.

She loves the rain, it hides her pain,

Something so wild is hard to tame.

Wild and free, she tries to let things be,

She sees the colors of the beautiful sea.

Wishes and prayers, as the days go by,

She finds herself looking at the pale blue sky.

Questions seem to fill her head,

Questions that seem to have no end.

Why?

SURROUNDINGS

Quiet is everything,

Everything around you,

Silent are the whispers,

You hear surround you.

Secret are the paths,

Paths, you've chosen yourself,

Calm are the trees,

Trees who whisper, trying to help.

Confident is the water,

Streams and rivers around you,

Soft is the air,

That seems to wrap around you.

Restless are the spirits,

Spirits who were done wrong,

Hurt, are the lonely,

The lonely who didn't belong.

Happy are the dancers,

Dancers that spin around their energy,

Sweet are the angels,

Angels that are so heavenly.

Free are the birds,

Birds who can do anything,

Kind are the people,

The people who respect every being.

REGULATED

Once there was a girl,

Who wanted to be free.

She lived in a country,

As deceiving as it could be.

They said they'd give you freedom,

But everything was regulated.

After a while, you aren't so blind,

That you see the promises belated.

There will be no more I'm sorry,

That's just the way it will be.

The people who run the country,

Don't really care about you or me.

In their mind, it's all about money,

They know they have it all.

They don't need help from anybody,

But someday, they will take the fall.

Suddenly, their world will come,

Crashing down to their feet,

And they will come running to us,

While we sit and watch their defeat.

MINE

You don't know me,

So why do you try,

To bring me down,

With all your lies.

What you don't see,

Is I just don't care,

You're not important,

Because you're not there.

Your hypocrisy,

It seems to me,

Knows no bounds,

Within this reality.

The next time you talk,

Speak to yourself,

If it's directed to me,

You can show yourself out.

Silly little human,

You're not important,

This is my world,

You can't turn it.

FALL LIKE RAIN

Empty Eyes and your childish grins,

Fakes the twilight and lets us in,

First to fall and always last to fly,

Let's the innocence pass you by,

Fall like rain

Picking stars with those, shaking hands,

Leaves this time we borrowed tasting bland.

Have you learned to glide with little time to spare,

If these ghosts could fly, would you even care?

Fall like rain

TERROR

*** As first published in *Rhythms* a college literary magazine

I walk over a bridge on 112th Street, I feel the ground shake beneath me,

I wait for my cab, as I look up and down the street.

Everything is quiet and calm, too quiet and calm to be good.

An eerie feeling comes over me. I think to myself of the woods.

I think about a forest so quiet and so still,

How there is always something waiting lurking there,

Waiting to devour you, hurt you, or kill,

I feel terrified and cannot move.

My cab is here now, and as I get inside,

The driver has shock in his eyes.

I ask him what is going on today,

He tells me the world has changed.

Indeed, it has, when chaos grips me,

My heart I cannot feel, and my head is spinning.

I feel pain and shock and terror as well,

As I think about the loss of life, I yell.

. . .

My mind is spinning, I am numb,

What just happened affects all of us,

An act of hatred believed to be right,

It has taken too many good people's lives.

I am not terrified for myself at all,

But I can see myself trapped beneath a wall,

The ground is shaking and sounds so loud,

Everyone is screaming for everyone to get out.

The anger, the chaos, the hurt and the pain,

All because someone thought they were right, it rains,

Tears from the heavens, of sadness,

Because someone took so many lives, carelessness.

In the name of your religion, you take lives,

And you believe that this is right?

In the name of politics, a war is waged,

But it was innocent people who had to pay.

CHANGES

As the values, morals, and ethics of the past,

Slip by the majority. I swear I can hear them laugh.

What they don't see is that progress is subjective,

And for every "advance," there is yet something else lacking.

They so eagerly stuff their eyes with ridiculous drama,

Busily pretending they are doing more than the next one.

Giving up their freedoms, their rights, and their honor,

Forever in pursuit of fame, recognition, or the next largest offer.

WICKED PEOPLE

I wonder if people, in their wicked ways,

Ever stop to count their wicked days.

Do they ever feel the pain they caused?

Do they understand the feelings wrought?

What makes a person become a monster inside?

Perhaps it is the same thing that makes them hide.

For hide, indeed, the wicked people do.

They hide everything they would do to you.

Deep within themselves, they see only one way,

By hurt and torment or any other kind of pain.

Trusting no one because they cannot trust themselves,

Twisted by bitterness, creating their own hell.

Do you know the wicked things that you do?

Pushing everyone away so they will not see the truth.

Hurting those around you because you know no other way.

What will you do when you want them all to stay?

CAUGHT BY A SOFT HAND

Swirling on the wind like the leaves on a path,

Waiting to be caught by an ever-gentle hand.

WALK WITH ME

Walk with me.

I see you now.

See your face.

I see your frown.

Walk with me.

I see your smile.

I know you want.

To stay for a while.

Come stay by my side.

Don't leave me again.

I missed you so much.

This can't be the end.

LIFE IS TOO SHORT

You don't know how much time you have,

Or if the words you just spoke will be your last,

Or if you have time to make your dreams, come true someday

You might not, stop waiting for things to "fall in place".

If you're like me, making everyone else happy at your expense,

Stop for a moment and think, do you want to die like this,

It's okay to tell someone who is damaging you to take a hike.

No one is worth the years, that damage takes away from your life,

We don't know when it is that our number will be up,

And we waste all this time, trying not to feel, trying to be tough.

We accept people who add drama, negativity & hate instead of love.

When we should be finding people, that will instead build us up.

In a time where negativity and stress breeds lethal disease, like cancer.

We need to understand that light, love and being positive is the answer.

MY MOTHER'S DEMON

Down I fell, and my face swelled,

She didn't stop there; she pulled my hair,

She pulled and hit, but I only felt a bit,

She screamed and yelled like a demon from hell,

Her eyes were like ice; I had to pay the price.

She hit and hit 'til the demon went away,

It would come again another day.

It spread through her body and made her strong,

But killed her slowly it wasn't long.

The beating stopped because she sent me away,

But being away caused as much pain,

She died one night after a call from a loved one,

She died and left me here with no one.

. . .

Silly, it seems that I would want her back,

But her temper didn't used to be all that bad,

If I could have her without the demon,

I would be glad as ever to call it even.

BULLIES

When I have had enough of the world

Will I choose to take my life away from it?

When I have had enough of the cruelty

Will you see you had a part in the decision?

Are you blind? Can you see the pain you cause?

Perhaps you don't care, perhaps you're heartless after all.

In your world, do you see everything you do as right?

Are your insecurities so great you cannot acknowledge this plight?

I watched so many tear others down to feel better.

In times like that, I see despair deepen and take over.

Your venomous words are nothing but deadly poison.

If I left this world, you would be somewhat responsible, for those choices.

I accept I am not perfect, indeed I have many flaws.

Unlike you, I forever strive for perfection but short I always fall.

So quick you are to use them as deadly ammunition.

And I am tired of fighting; I'm so tempted to let you win.

Oh, the despair I have seen and felt from the cruelty.

The lives already lost gone forever over nothing,

Beautiful people with wonderful hearts, perhaps naive.

Wanting only love, taking their lives because you don't see.

DISAPPEAR

If I disappear and you don't see me,

It's because I had to unplug myself to be free.

If I disappear into the night,

It's that I drove away to make things right.

If I don't return home,

Perhaps I found someplace where I am not alone.

I AM MY MOTHER'S DAUGHTER

I am my mother's daughter.

I am proud to be just that.

I miss her and love her every day.

But nothing can change the facts.

She left one day and won't come back.

Taken by evil, and I want her back.

Despite the hurt and pain she caused.

Her heart was good despite her flaws.

I am my mother's daughter.

Still, in some way, I try not to be.

My rage is suppressed far more than she,

And manipulation does not come easily.

I try each day to improve my life,

Taking life lessons and growing from strife.

I tried to grow where she was not allowed the time.

I try to be better, but I cannot see the line.

I am my mother's daughter.

Complete with flaws and insecurities.

I wonder sometimes how it should be.

But the fact remains I am undeniably me.

I look just like she did, with a slight difference.

I have her pain and temper to deal with.

Still, the hate I once had in my heart is gone,

And I have grown where she could not.

Still, I am my mother's daughter,

For all that it might imply.

I no longer deny it; I no longer fight,

She was a strong woman, as am I.

ACQUIESCENCE TO MADNESS

Do not mistake my silence for acquiescence to your madness.

I will not defend myself to lies, or give away your secrets.

I have no need to engage in the war largely within your mind.

Though you may spew venom, I will not make it mine.

Understand that I had accepted you for who you were.

So, I should not have been surprised to hear your words.

You speak of things you yourself have been doing,

And twist the truth as if to stop your insecurities from growing.

You may never know the truth of who I truly am inside.

Indeed, this likely wouldn't interest someone so ready to lie.

I have heard the words you once spoke twisted to your end,

And I have seen the darkened moods shifting with the wind.

I have kept your secrets and your abusive nature to myself.

I have learned of things said, and I know who you talked about.

With a heavy heart, I will walk away from it all with great sadness,

But never mistake my silence for acquiescence to your madness.

HOUSE OF CARDS

I feel as though I am trapped within a house of cards,

That could collapse at any moment; life seems exceedingly hard.

One wayward whisper and it would come down,

One careless gesture is all it takes to knock it all to the ground.

I feel as if it were built in the middle of the city

With feet trampling all about, everyone carrying carelessly.

I feel as though I'm running, trying to hold each card up,

Fearing a point, with every passerby, I won't be strong enough.

Each card represents a different area of my life,

One for each area that is a mess, As I struggle to make it right.

I'm in a house of cards, struggling to survive

Every waking moment, using everything I've got to stay alive.

DEMONS

Suddenly, I let the demons run free in my mind,

Once locked safely in a chest, tucked away in the darkness,

Now they're roaming free, tainting everything they touched,

Bitterness, anger, rage, and a deep sorrow filled with loss.

Of all the feelings I had, sorrow was the most powerful,

It consumed me in a way that was deceptively comforting,

It's like a blanket of soft darkness wrapping you so tight,

You don't know it's suffocating you; it's stealing your light.

Hand in hand with sorrow came loss, deep and vast loss,

Reminding me of what they had stolen and who was stolen,

I wade through dark waters that look like memories in my mind,

I could see them, daisy-chained together, pulling me in quicksand.

Then the bitterness, at why these things happened to me,

Sarcastically screaming, why was I the one so damned lucky,

Damned perhaps, why, when others get to live without this pain,

Did I have to endure and struggle to be more, to be enough just being me.

Because I am a survivor and many of them are not?

Maybe it's because a lesser person would have died.

Or at least their light would? Perhaps it's to prove that I am stronger than all of that?

But I'd still gladly set my past, on fire and watch it burn to death, screaming.

And there is the anger and rage I used to be so well acquainted,

Hello, my old friends, thank you for saving my life once again,

I'm sorry I tried to stuff you away in a dark corner because I was afraid,

But the intensity is so great, that I feared it would overwhelm me completely.

WHAT SAY YOU

What say you, you who would sit on your throne made of paper and look down on me,

Yet when you sit on that throne, it would crumble and fold and you are left alone.

Go forward with your life and lies, spouting words you know nothing of.

Continue down your path of self-righteous deception, keep ignoring, and fight reflection.

What say you, you who stand on your soap box ready to condemn those who know you,

For fear that they may see, into your soul and seek out your fears as you do to them.

Go forward with your life, blind to the possibilities that those you condemn can help.

Continue on your path of destruction, all the while convinced it is your salvation.

What say you, you who would hurt me simply because I embody everything you desire.

Yet you do not realize, everything I am has cost me a price you could never understand,

Go forward in your ignorance, for I would not wish my past on my worst enemy.

Continue down your path, while looking down your nose, but you will never know me.

What say you, you who has tried to play the victim all the while knowing that you are not,

You only crave attention, rooted in your past, and seek to distract others from the cause.

Go forward, with your life and know you are living a lie that hurts many others.

Continue down your path, of self-destruction, all the while thinking it is your salvation.

What say you, you who have torn me to pieces with words of a thousand swords?

How much more venom can you spew at me, seeking to keep me down on the floor?

Go forward as if your words do not inflict real wounds, yet knowing that they do.

Continue down your path of egotistical self-satisfaction that instead leaves you empty.

What say you, you who has twisted and turned tables to avoid looking within yourself?

How many more friends will you hurt while you try desperately to avoid figuring it out?

Go forward in your life for there will come a time when the situation will force you.

Continue down your path of duplicity and shallow face values that change as the winds do.

What say you, you who know me, do you count yourself as friend or foe, do you know?

Do you know that I will never ask you to choose, never ask you for more than you have?

Go forward with your lives. I love you all for exactly who you are good, bad, and neutral.

Continue down your paths to happiness and love and find everything you were meant to.

CAN'T SLEEP

I was exhausted, my mind was spent,

Yet here it is, racing while I lie in bed.

RAVING MIND

Sit on the shore and watch the waves,

No one ever knows the thoughts that rave.

Inside your mind and through your heart,

Everything in your life is being torn apart.

No one loves, and no truths; everyone lies to get through.

No silence, no screaming, it's all on you,

To leave and go would be easier still,
But it's the hard way you learned and the hard way you will.

Sorry for all these things left unsaid,

Apologies not accepted and the dying undead.

No more you will cry with a smile on your face,

The pain is difficult in this world of fast pace.

The truth of the matter is never told,

While all the people now are growing old.

Too tired to get up and too sad to see,

The world runs on through ancient mystery.

Sad to go and sad to live,

You're stuck in the middle of everything.

Wish for and pray for the end and beginning,

But never mind the thoughts that keep on ringing.

ORPHAN

I am an orphan, wait you'll see,

I was an orphan the day my mom left me.

My father, never really came around,

My dad gave up and fooled around.

I lost my dad when he and mom split,

I had two sisters, and he would visit with them,

He stopped taking me, and I didn't know why,

But he took them and not me, and I cried, and I cried.

That was one parent that wasn't real,

The other just didn't know how to be there,

So, my mom was dying and sent me away,

To go meet my father, and there I would stay.

Here was a man that I never knew,

But she sent me to him; what could I do,

So, I cried, and I was angry, but away I flew,

Up to a place with horrors all new.

On the way, I thought he would be a prince,

But he was broken, and our ties not thick,

And his structure, well, it just did not exist,

And the real reason I was here; obligations.

So here is a man who is my father by blood,

But he was never there, and I thought my dad was,

I would get closer and be pushed far away,

I kept trying, it seemed, it was just my way.

My relationships, seemed, to mirror this madness,

It took a long time to figure out the root of my distress,

I kept trying to please, and trying to be loved,

But there came a day when I realized it was all for not.

I lost my dad the day my mom sent me away,

My father was not there because she tried to keep me safe,

And I lost my mom to cancer at the age of fifteen,

I became an orphan that day; it was obvious to me.

BALANCE RESTORED

She stood in the shadows alone, watching the fire burn,

All the evil that had ever touched her,

Finally, she welcomed the darkness in her soul,

Finally, justice was served, and balance was restored.

SERVE AND PROTECT

I see you with your hand on your gun,

Ready to react at a moment's notice for one of us.

I see you with your eyes darting everywhere,

There is no downtime for you; you must always be aware.

TRADE-OFFS

As the values, morals, and ethics of the past,

Slip by the majority; I swear I can hear them laugh.

What they don't see is that progress is subjective,

And for every "advance," there is yet something else lacking.

They so eagerly stuff their eyes with ridiculous drama,

Busily pretending they are doing more than the next one.

Giving up their freedoms, their rights, and their honor,

All the while they put up a face, pretending to be noble.

THE STORM

I awoke to the sound of howling wind suddenly and intensely,

My first thought: I wish my love were here to share this with me,

The cyclone outside wrapped around me as I sat in the center safe,

And the wind swirling around me continuously absorbed my rage.

In that moment of reflection, I realized that is what my love does for me,

He wraps me safely in his arms and absorbs my rage diligently,

He buffers me from the world, placing himself in the line of fire,

Wrapping me in a cocoon that allows me to, once again, feel desire.

He does all of this without even knowing how he affects my internal tides,

It happens naturally, and I swear he has the sun shining from his eyes,

I see that light; I see it even when he cannot believe it could be,

And I feel the fire of the earth's core within him when he holds me.

When the storm clouds amass, and the sky turns those shades of grey,

I am not like the others wrapped in their sleepy mediocrity for the day,

Instead, I can feel the sparks in my eyes, and my world is electrified,

I'm filled with a strange calm, an intensity, and a fire that burns deep inside.

The rain, when it started, felt like bullets searing through my very soul,

Tearing and ripping through my emotions, my mind urging me to let go,

There I am in the center of it; this moment I'm completely alone,

Yet I am strangely comforted, calm, somehow intensified, as I realize:

I am the storm.

AFTER TWILIGHT

It was in the late hours, after twilight,

That she realized she was completely alone.

It was after the moon had crested and started to fall,

She realized she had no one to turn to at all.

RISK IT ALL

Your fragility,

It seems to me,

Shows the world your humanity.

Those who falter,

Accepting pain as they begin to fall,

They are the chosen few who risk it all.

TORN AND TATTERED BITS

Sometimes at night, I hear them,

The ghosts from my past,

They bring me torn and tattered bits,

From times, that have long since passed.

WOUNDED

Maybe after you recharge you'll be okay,

Maybe after you sleep you'll be ready today.

Perhaps you just got a little too excited and talked to much,

Or maybe you just couldn't help spilling all your thoughts,

But now you are afraid you are just a little too much,

You're battling lifelong stories about being too much or not enough,

If we all come into this world alone then why does it matter,

I'm suddenly craving being held as I sit alone tears splatter,

It's been years since I let some hold me or offer connection,

But now I simultaneously crave it, Yet I'm terrified to let anyone in,

Floating in the pool it hits me I'm battling that abandonment,

I'm not sure I can survive another loss, so I just reject the possibility of it.

That means I expect everyone to leave or worse attack me,

So my guard is always up, never relaxing, never allowed to just be,

I'm always talking about healing, trauma and grief,

Yet, here I sit looking at my wounds judging myself harshly,

I've been isolated so long I didn't have this opportunity,

To see my opened wound and how it had festered in my retreat,

From the rest of the world for a few years in my deepest grief.

THE MISFIT MAIDEN

She's a bit too sensitive,

The nun said over the phone.

My mom, to her credit,

Said that's how she was born.

A few years later, it's still the same,

She's made the honor roll again,

It's just such a shame,

She's far too sensitive.

My mother would sigh,

As she put the phone to the receiver,

She accepted that I cried,

And felt everything a little deeper.

It was not just in school,

I was different from everyone,

I would gravitate towards misfits,

Happy to be their champion.

No one really knows why,

Nature or nurture,

A traumatic past gone awry,

A miss-wired brain or nerve?

Only one thing was certain,

I was a little bit off,

Not quite like the others,

Perhaps a little too soft.

As I progressed through life,

To others, it became obvious,

With a mounting strive,

Though I remained fairly oblivious.

With no one to protect me,

And society's lack of understanding,

Predators would come to see,

An easy mark for mishandling.

Luckily oblivion helped,

It kept me dancing around,

Unaware of the damage wrought,

I was still able to rebound.

Still, all that damage simmered,

Deep below the protections,

My mind would still shiver,

At the hidden recollections.

How fortunate I was to want to heal,

To seek out help and counsel,

When things were less than ideal,

Even when things felt utterly doubtful.

I don't know if I was born this way,

With this burning desire to grow,

Or if it happened out of necessity,

Or even a byproduct of hope.

It might come as a surprise.

That something good could be bad,

A positive mindset weaponized,

Warped to excuse the mad and sad.

While others, less willing to grow,

Dumped all their issues over me,

I eventually came to know,

The risk of thinking so differently.

I started to see, but only over time,

The price I was paying for avoidance,

Of too many things in my mind,

That should have been more annoying.

As I started to slowly accept,

Both my differences and past events,

I could begin to heal instead of deflect,

Accepting that I'm different from most of the rest.

THE MISFIT MOTHER

You are not a real mother,

You didn't give birth.

That is what some people said,

When I took in a boy and a girl.

You are not a real mother,

You're just their aunt,

But when you make a mistake,

They will call you out like a mom.

You are not a real mother,

If you are too young,

You are not a real mother,

If you are not young enough.

You are not a real mother,

You can't be, you're single,

You are not a real mother,

You need help being financially stable.

You are not a real mother,

That is how they made me feel,

For so many reasons,

But not one of them was real.

I was a real mother,

The day I took that call,

When they told me I had a choice,

I didn't falter at all.

I was a real mother,

When I took in those two kids,

And I was a real mother,

When I did my very best.

I was a real mother,

I cried just like all the rest,

When I wasn't sure I was right,

When I tried to hide all my stress.

I was a real mother,

I loved them with all my heart,

I tried to teach them everything they'd need,

To one day make a successful start.

I was a real mother.

When I grieved the loss,

When I questioned myself,

Trying to figure out where I went wrong.

I was a real mother,

When she grew up and left,

When I felt the emptiness in my chest,

As I learned about the empty nest.

I was a real mother,

I know I wasn't perfect,

Don't tell me it wasn't real.

I was a mother, on purpose.

THE MISFIT CRONE

There is no such thing as a misfit crone,

This archetype has to shed any imposter syndrome,

Empowered and ready to fully accept her role.

Certain that she will learn ever more as she goes.

Though it may be a rocky transition from mother to crone,

She sees life as providing endless possibilities to grow,

She realizes she doesn't shed the mother aspect of her soul,

And instead expands, offering it to the world as a whole.

Society may treat the crone like a misfit,

They don't understand and tend to dismiss it,

Completely obsessed with the fountain of youth

They are missing critical components that make up you.

The crone has accepted she is not lacking,

She is still the maiden, capable of dancing and laughing,

She is still the mother but with a little less nagging,

She has become all three; her intuition surpassing.

Coming fully into herself and all that she is,

The maiden and the mother are fully part of her, she understands.

She is all three, and she has learned so much through the years,

Now is her time to shine, not to disappear.

The world needs the wisdom that the crone can bring forth,

She won't offer advice unsolicited, so she waits for you to explore.

Offering her love to the maiden, the mother and herself, the crone,

She is on an everlasting journey to help herself and others grow.

Your Misfit Free-Writing

YOUR MISFIT FREE-WRITING

Have you ever felt like a misfit, like you didn't quite belong? Have you ever seen someone that seemed like a misfit to you that caught your attention? I invite you to write about your experiences or observations.

Your Misfit Poem(s)

YOUR MISFIT POEM(S)

Read through your free writing and look for any poetry in it. Sometimes circling words that rhyme can help you see patterns. Use it as inspiration to write your own misfit poems, or just let the poetry flow through you.

Misuse and Abuse

No one expects it,
Everyone wants to pretend,
It'll never happen.

It's a difficult topic no one wants to talk about it, but abuse is something we should all talk about. There were times I had a very difficult time reconciling the damage that I had to repair. In some cases, it was clear; in others, my mind would get stuck in a cycle of blame. I broke the cycle when I acknowledged that much of what broke me down or damaged me came from incompatibility. It led me to a strong belief that people become toxic when they try to force incompatible relationships. Blame didn't serve me, but healing and learning did. Still, I had to go through it, sometimes over and over again. Until I learned valuable lessons. I took my pain and turned it into poetry to process it. This chapter is filled with vulnerability as I found myself making poor decisions. Perhaps some of these poor decisions were from a lack of healthy examples or my people-pleasing, chameleon tendencies. If these poems resonate with you, I'm sorry you know this pain. Please know you can come out the other side and love again.

QUIET WHISPERS

Silent are my screams that speak of heartache.

Silent are the prayers that I dare to make.

Quiet are the whispers that I speak to myself.

Quiet are the secrets that I hold inside my heart.

Silenced are the echoes that tell my story in bold.

Silenced are the sparrows that helped me through it all.

Secret are the scares left behind by heartache.

Secret is the pain that my lover truly makes.

Silent are the birds on this of saddest days.

Silent are the trees that hide the sun's rays.

Silent is the pain from a love so devastating.

Silent is the recovery that I intend to make.

SORRY

Sorry to stay and,

Sorry, you're gone,

Sorry, I missed you,

You've been gone for so long.

Happy to see you,

Sad to talk with you,

Happy to be with you,

Sad that you left me blue.

Awake at night and,

Asleep during the day,

Nothing makes me happy,

Unless I see you today.

Sorry, you're gone and,

Sorry, I'm here,

I didn't want things,

To be as they appear.

Sad that you left me,

Sorry, you don't care,

Sad you're away from me,

I have nothing left here.

Too lonely to fight,

Too sad to argue,

I wish you understood,

Just how much I love you.

ANGERED

Angered by your silly ways,

Sometimes saddened for many days,

You love her but cannot have her,

So, you turn to walk my way.

You came to me with a broken heart,

You want happiness to be a new start,

You're with me, but you love her,

Sooner or later, I'll get hurt.

I care for you more than you know,

But I cannot be with you if you love her so,

My silent cries will stay that way,

My secrets guard themselves every day.

You will never know how I feel,

I hope and wish your wounds will heal,

Wishing you were here, hoping that I'm there,

Never knowing where you'll be, your life was never fair.

I've learned this through the years,

The path is never smooth, not even for you.

NOT THAT YOU CARE

Not that you care,

But I wanted to talk,

Not that you care,

I'm going for a walk.

I know sometimes you do,

And sometimes it doesn't matter,

I know the way you think,

When you think something's the matter.

Not that you care,

I would give my life for you,

Not that you care,

Sometimes, you make me feel blue.

I feel like you're not there,

And you never wanted to be,

I feel like I'm alone sometimes,

But then I know you love me.

Not that you care,

You made me so angry,

Not that you care,

But you really do love me.

ONCE MORE

I trusted you once more, to slam my face in the door,

I believed you one more time, and let you comfort my soul,

Now, the feeling of being used is back with a vengeance,

It won't be denied; it feels as though you planned this.

You always knew when I was vulnerable, what I would believe,

Taking advantage of the goodness ingrained deep within me.

Always, I took away or searched for something that would help me,

And always when you would leave, I would feel as though you betrayed me.

You tried to fix me when I thought I was broken,

I just needed something to help me grow some,

You helped me grow and caused me pain

This bittersweet relationship is insane.

The saying goes, fool me once, fool me twice,

But I let you make a fool of me for a third time,

How many people think I'm insane to make it to three,

And even I wonder sometimes, after everything, how can I be so naive

TRUST

 So, you lied, just like they all do,

They all lie for different reasons,

But the reasons are all selfish,

Still, they want you to believe them.

They lie and say it's to protect you.

They don't want you to be hurt,

But I've known this as a child,

They always put themselves first.

I haven't had the pleasure,

To know an honest man,

Instead, I've known the bad ones,

And a few who raised their hands.

I've been beaten, dragged, and left,

And yet here I still stand,

Because I'm stronger than your lies,

Let me show my poker hand.

I'm tired of being lied to,

Because I believe in being good,

I'm sick of being called naive,

Because I expect you to act like you should.

Maybe I have daddy issues,

They lied, and abandoned us both,

They sure didn't set a good example,

My mother, and I left broken souls.

So, you go tell yourself your story,

Try to convince yourself and then me,

Tell the whole world your lies,

But I'm done trusting in things I can't see.

The saddest thing of all,

Is that you took away that trust,

You took it with all your lies,

Without trust, I don't know if I can love.

NO LONGER A VICTIM

*** Awarded the Editor's Choice Award by the International Library of Poetry

Once is enough to be raped and beaten down,

But to go through it repeatedly should not be allowed.

I was stronger because I had lived through it before,

But still, those issues have created many doors.

So many walls and doors locked tightly shut,

That I am surprised I am still capable of love.

Still and silent, I sit here and wonder why,

And how no one knew what happened those times.

Did you really confuse rape with love?

When I said no, and you refused to stop?

Did you really think that it was all just a game?

When you had me by the throat and threw me away?

When will you see that what you did was wrong?

Even though it did succeed in making me strong.

Never again will I feel so much pain,

I will not ever be a victim again.

BELIEVED IN A DREAM

Too bad you dreamed of romance,

All good things simply don't last.

It's simple, really, you believed in a dream,

But now you realize dreams are not meant to be.

Sad, I thought I could have happiness,

But now, all I feel is a bitter loneliness.

I am trapped in a world so terribly cruel,

And I always thought that I could count on you.

But you are never there when I need you the most,

It's not your fault; there's just no time for us.

No, it must be my fault; you've said it yourself,

You put it all on me, and I have no help.

What I wanted will never come to pass,

The one I love, I can never really have.

So many things that you have left to do,

I'm just in the way; what happened to me and you.

HURT AGAIN

I thought about surprising him, but I am too afraid.

Every time I do, it seems something gets in the way.

I dress to get his attention and hold it close,

But when I go through it all, I could be a ghost.

The rejection is clear to me, and it causes so much pain,

I wonder why I bothered to make us a special day.

I think of ways to surprise him and how he will feel,

But always, I end up hurt again, and I don't think it heals.

I want to have a day where everything goes right,

The candles are lit, my dress, night, and the moon is bright tonight.

I can never have this because I won't be hurt again.

So, I will play dress up and cry once more because of him.

I suppose I should not have expected anything,

But I cannot help feeling all these feelings.

I know that he will probably never understand,

Some say that this is simply because he is a man.

I think that perhaps it is because it doesn't happen to him,

Because I know in my heart, I will always keep letting him in.

CHOICES

*** Awarded the Editor's Choice Award by the International Library of
Poetry

A broken trust, can it mend?

Or should I leave it and start again?

Can I have trust at all?

I wonder about this as I fall.

Once I fell, and I was caught,

Only to feel myself drop.

If I fall, who will catch me,

Will anyone be there to see?

Doubt and chaos reign supreme,

Just what is it he wants from me?

He confuses me with subtlety,

Why did I stay when I felt I should leave?

Your kindness and understanding,

Perhaps another is too demanding,

Maybe I do not want what I thought,

Perhaps, this was the lesson taught.

Will you see me as I fall?

I cannot seem to slow down at all,

A plethora of confusion and doubt,

What is this all about?

STILL, I AM NOT FREE

*** Awarded the Editor's Choice Award by the International Library of Poetry

I have drifted into a deep slumber,

My dreams offer me no comfort,

In this world and the next, he haunts me,

Forever reminding me,

That still, I am not free.

WICKED HEART

Capable of a love that cuts deep in my soul,

Why must I suffer this pain all alone?

Trapped by my desire to have something real,

Tortured by a heart that I cannot steal.

Lost in a dream of romance and true love,

Awakened by the truth, there is none of the above,

Stricken by the notion that my dreams are lies,

Tortured by this reality, these tears I cry.

Wicked is the heart that leaves me this way,

Evil is the notion that has crept in and stays,

Lost am I, with my heart beating ever so slow,

Waiting to be wrong, but I know it is not so.

NOT LOVE

What is this anguish I have caused myself?

Allowing you to twist me up and all around.

How much of myself did I really lose?

Letting you tear me apart, leaving me bruised.

Doubting myself, you had me relying on you.

I couldn't do anything without feeling like a fool.

Now that you're gone, I have slowly come back to me,

I started to understand these changes were made subtly.

I started to identify what I really loved within myself.

I understood I created for myself this little personal hell.

As if suddenly, I just didn't deserve the love I craved.

You had me believe that kind of love was only a game.

Now I can see the truth of it all: my love still exists.

You only succeeded in creating doubt for a little bit.

I know that there is someone that will come into my life.

Someone who, instead of clouds, brings light into my life.

ACCEPT

I see you for who you are, and I accept,

Though you are emotional and erratic,

I will still be there because you are a friend.

I see you for who you are, and I accept,

Though you are sometimes cruel and rash,

I was there because you were my friend.

I see you for who you are, and I accept,

Your venomous words and bottled-up rage,

I believed you, the friend you pretended.

I see you for who you are, and I accept,

Your actions and words ring clear and true,

You were my enemy masquerading as a friend.

I see you for who you are, and I accept,

Consumed by yourself you did not know me,

I'm not sure why you would pretend.

I see you for who you are, and I accept,

I would have always accepted you for yourself,

Yet it is who I am that you chose to reject.

I see you for who you are, and I accept,

Our differences cannot be reconciled.

Your existence has become circumspect.

I see you for who you are, and I accept,

I know beautiful souls that love all of me,

With them, I need not be defensive.

ONLY FOR US

If you could only see him the way that I see him,

You would know why I love him the way I do.

But you will never see those sides of him,

Because they are meant only for me, never for you.

If you could see me the way he sees me,

You would know why it is that we fit,

But you will never see those sides of me,

Because they are not meant for you, only for him.

SOFT

When she dances and twirls in the moonlight, do you see?

She shines with a hidden and darkened inner beauty.

She wants comfort and yearns for a soft caress,

She holds true to her ideals and waits in the darkness.

Someone stripped her of her softness and light heart,

She had to learn not to let someone in just to hurt.

Still, she dances and twirls with a grace thought lost,

And she hopes for the day she can shed all that's false.

Safe once before, secure and then torn apart,

Her fears are founded in reality, not her heart.

ABUSED

I've been hit with fists, and I've been hit with words,

There is little difference; both caused great hurt,

And the next day, there is always some apology,

He says it won't happen again; that's just not me.

Hit dragged me down the stairs, and lifted me by my throat,

If you think I will take it, you'll find out that I won't.

The emotional hits, now those are much worse,

It's hard to see them coming, and hard to see the hurt.

Manipulation, mind games, and then the controlling,

I'm not sure which way it is that I should be going.

From the outside, they look in awe and wonder,

How could she stay and make such a blunder?

Their ignorance and lack of understanding prove,

That you can't understand what you have not gone through,

I pray they never know, and yet wish they understood,

I didn't look for this, and I fought it when I could.

The saddest thing of all is that I just wanted to be loved,

I had lost so many people that I didn't recognize a dud.

So willing was I, to give my heart away,

I chose the wrong fellow and made a grave mistake.

You might look at someone and wonder why they stay,

I look at them, and I can't help but pray; oh heavens do I pray.

I pray that they realize their self-worth before it is too late,

I pray that one day, they find the courage and support to no longer stay.

TRYING AGAIN

He held me, and at that moment I felt safe,

He squeezed me, and at that moment I felt wanted,

He kissed me, and at that moment, I reveled in the sensation,

My mind, unable to poison the moment I wish could have lasted forever.

His fingers traced my face with such softness and care,

So much more than I had felt over the last few years.

Every touch is electric, soft, and caring with hints of passion under the surface.

I could no longer tell how much of what I felt was real.

This could be a dream that easily turned into a nightmare,

My mind is active once more on the border of despair.

I've opened the door, and I threw it open with wild abandon,

Now, would I be rewarded, or would something terrible happen?

It's too soon to judge, too close to call, but my demons have come awake,

And their only desire is to ensure that in love, I do not fall,

They revel in my darkness and try to snuff away my light,

Remind me of the torment and bring to the surface my desire for flight.

It's an insidious, winding evil to make me relive such horrors,

Just as I felt I might be safe, I was reminded of the others,

Battered, bruised, and left after they took what they wanted,

Could I leave the door open again? Tell me, why should I bother?

It was worse this time; the memories were somehow more,

Things that I was not ready to face came tumbling through the door,

I'll be damned if I let them steal away my goodness and my light,

I may be battered, bruised, and afraid, but I won't give up the fight.

I fell asleep feeling safe but woke up in such a panic,

The darkness that surrounded me stole my breath in pieces,

Was I safe? Were the children, how could I let this happen,

I know better; it's been too long and not long enough all at once.

DEMONS AND MONSTERS

I spent so much time with demons,

That the monsters somehow seemed okay.

I was covered in so many scars and wounds,

That the absence of violence made me feel safe.

I found myself looking at the monsters,

Not knowing what they truly were, not seeing their true face.

I found myself trapped in a different kind of hell than the demons built,

But it seemed best, so I'd stay.

But the monsters ripped me apart, just like the demons used to do,

And I ended up broken and bruised all the same.

There is a certain kind of peace when you know you've had enough,

A clarity that comes with knowing you are done.

BROKEN LOVE

From love that heals to love that cuts,

He brings me from pleasure to a puddle of tears and blood.

From healing my heart and making it whole,

To clawing through it, ripping it apart once more.

I believed in fate, I believed in love,

But he twisted me, and I forgot where I was.

His kind heart battled with his demons,

Then he would cut me to my soul with his words, as they won.

But it's really all me, all in my head,

I allowed this; I allowed these feelings once again.

I'm all wrong; that's the way it is,

I am made up of mistakes, pain, and carelessness.

I'm too hard to love and love the wrong ones,

And the price I've paid has been my sanity and love.

BLACK AND BLUE

Bruises black and blue turned.

To green and yellow over time,

But there were deeper wounds,

On the heart, soul, and mind.

Fear of being bruised,

Was never a primary feeling,

But being abused by love,

Is something else entirely.

I can take the pain inflicted

Carelessly to my body,

But the words were subtler,

They almost got by me,

Even that, I could handle, even that,

I could heal, or I could ignore,

I could not accept that someone I loved,

Could so easily cut me to the core.

STUCK IN A MEMORY

I'm stuck in a memory, and I'm only half in this world,

I'm stuck reliving the pain that I could once barely endure,

I'm stuck in a memory, and it's hard to tell what's real,

Because everything is a hazy shade, and I'm stuck in this movie reel.

If you've never had a trauma, you could never know.

How it feels to be stuck in this awful sort of limbo.

If you've, you never lived it, you can't really understand,

My memory is failing me because it's lost in a past land.

FICKLE DEMONS

These Fickle demons haunt me,

At their leisure, they sneer and taunt me.

They come for me entwined in memories,

In the darkness, they gain power and drag me to sea.

Plummeting in the depths of the ocean,

Surrounded by frigid waters and darkness, scars open,

These fickle demons are tricksters by nature.

Tainting my memories, they reached inside and changed them,

They come out of nowhere when I'm unprepared,

They come when I'm happy; they feed on despair,

These fickle demons that plagued my past,

They keep trying to win me, they keep holding fast,

But I'm not as weak as I let them think,

I've grown comfortable in darkness so I can rise after I sink.

PIECES OF ME, GONE

Innocence, I held onto it with everything I had,

Believing in fairies and magic drifting into another land,

But demons feed on light, seeking to seal as much as they can hold,

And I was no match at such a young age for someone so old.

Pieces of me, gone, blackened by their touch,

Consumed in darkness, bereft of any love.

The stage was set now for others to come,

Permission to use me, as shown by the absence of love.

So, I believed in another world drastically different in my mind,

And I lost memories and vast, darkened spaces of time,

Willfully, my mind manipulated so very many facts,

Trying to keep me safe, trying to prevent that fatal snap.

Magic, it seems, existed, for me, at least,

I refused to give it up, refused to let it leave,

There were days I survived on sheer spite alone,

I wouldn't let them take any more than they had taken before.

I know the evils of this world; I've seen some firsthand,

But I won't let them turn me into darkness or turn me into them.

HE BROKE ME

He broke me,

I don't believe he intended to,

Though I, ever naive,

Tend to make up excuses for everybody.

PIECES OF ME

I want to tell you everything.

I want to show you, my very soul,

Although I feel you see it,

You saw through me on your own.

You were so familiar with the darkness,

And I was in denial that it existed.

You fell in love with me for my light,

And I was afraid my darkness would kill it.

I'M STILL WITH YOU

I'm still with you, but you feel so far away,

I'm changing all the stations that remind me,

We used to be another way.

Now I'm feeling so alone. You said we'd be partners, but now you're gone.

You've become something else, and now

I've got to move on.

I'm still with you, but you can't show me love,

I'm feeling lost and alone,

And I feel like I'm not the only one,

I'm still with you, but you've changed who you are,

Once romantic, you'd do all the things they never did,

You set the bar.

I'm still with you, clinging to hope I'm wrong.

I'm doing everything to stay,

Hoping you'll come along

TRICKED

I was that bad chick,

Without ever realizing, tricked,

He told me how it was and wasn't,

And I believed it.

Oh, he had me doing things that he knew full well I didn't believe in.

When I found out the truth,

What could I do?

He'd already given me a black eye, not a nice guy, it's true.

So, I left him anyway because that is what girls are supposed to do.

And when he lied again, telling me it wasn't true,

I left anyway and said we could be friends. I was a fool.

BATTLE-HARDENED

Battle Hardened at home,

Almost dead three times over.

Broke free to save my friend,

Uncertain if it all mattered in the end.

Put myself at risk for others daily,

Without the status you knew proudly.

You said be proud of what I'd been through,

And yet, my service means nothing to you.

My battle wounds rendered meaningless,

Because they didn't come from your service.

I didn't do it for the glory,

Something center stage in your story.

I never expected a thank you, I just acted.

Driven to do what is right, justice enacted.

Holding to my own code of honor through the pain,

That's the difference, you couldn't survive the same,

You're not as honorable as you claimed.

FIRST LOVE

There was no tenderness or gentle love,

He had a persona I became quickly in awe of.

It was an enchantment mean to ensnare me.

His goal to control me without me seeing.

Like a moth to the flame I flew yearning,

Unaware of the dangers that were looming.

In my youth so blissfully unaware and unassuming.

Wanting only to be cherished and loved unconditionally.

He had found the perfect victim, so insecure and already broke,

From the fatherless homes I had lived to the ones that came before,

I was perfect for him to manipulate and mold,

He relished the idea of making me his to behold,

He sought to destroy me, so I would never leave.

Believing that through his charade, I would never see.

But his lack of tenderness and acts of brute force,

Eventually pushed me past the illusions and I changed course.

No longer content to be the victim or handle his lack of remorse,

I knew I had to free myself even if by my *own* brute force.

PACKING UP

I've decided, now that you are gone.

To put myself first and spend time alone.

After all that we have been through.

I guess I'll do me, and you'll do you.

And now I'm packing up my life with you,

Something I never thought I'd do.

Among the words spoken, unkind,

Made your choice to leave me behind.

While I know I'll always love you,

Life together seemed perpetually cruel.

Perhaps I should've been the one to leave,

But then again, that just wouldn't be me.

I wish neither of us had to live through pain,

Some say it's just life; it's just that way.

I wish you all the best wherever you go,

I hope you remember; that you reap what you sow.

INTERNAL LOVERS WOUNDS

Distant and disappointed in me, he lashed out,

Believing he was rightfully going about.

Hurt, he would punish others sometimes silently,

Believing in punishment and holding steadfast to his beliefs.

Never seeing the internal damage his behavior caused.

Believing the only true facts were the ones he himself saw.

Deep within he often believed everyone else was at fault.

This was the only way he could ensure he was absolved.

SEEKING WHAT WAS

One of the saddest things I've seen,

That turns love bittersweet,

Is when a significant other,

Withholds love from the other.

Pushing them down low,

Delighted to dull their glow,

Sometimes unaware of their deeds,

Done to fill an unknowable need.

Turning passion and safety dark,

Creating a jail where they are the guard,

Feeding themselves off the pain,

While the other clings to whatever remains,

Searching for the love that once was,

Seeking to return to what once was love.

CURIOUSLY COMMON

*** As previously published in Amazon Best Seller 100 Poems and Possibilities for Healing

It's a curious thing, to know so many suffered as I did.

How could something so brutal become so common.

Molded and shaped to accept brutish behavior and make excuses,

I remember feeling like I couldn't possibly recover from the abuses.

Childhood scars seemed to dictate my action without my understanding,

Propelling me into more situations that would further scar me.

The alternative was to embrace it and become what they called me,

And embrace the abuse, their definition and the depravity.

It's interesting looking back after trauma therapy has succeeded,

From a lens that isn't jaded or warped or misleading.

I deserved love, yes, but, I deserved to learn to love myself.

Yet I struggled for most of my life figuring this out.

The risk of overcorrecting and becoming jaded was real,

I didn't want to be bitter and hateful, a balance would be ideal.

But my mistrust for the type of people that taken so much,

Often lead to me putting up walls and using them as a crutch.

It was easier for me to isolate myself than to put myself out there,

And risk being wrong and end up in another nightmare.

After a few failed attempts at finding a healthy relationships,

I decided to put it all on hold until I could heal more from this.

As I healed and learned more about loving myself authentically,

I started to set standards and learn healthy boundaries.

I learned that it isn't selfish to put your needs over someone's wants,

And taking care of yourself starts with your own thoughts.

I slowly began to learn more about self compassion,

And how to talk to myself with more affection.

The truth is if you wouldn't say the same things to some you care for,

You don't deserve to have them said to you any more.

Next I leaned in on gratitude practices daily,

Finding three things to be grateful for should be easy.

I learned the subtle art of self forgiveness,

Not a small feat for a devout perfectionist.

I learned that I need people around me that want to grow,

Because I'll never stop wanting to learn more.

There was a time I wasn't sure I'd ever survive,

But now I know we all have it in us to rise.

So I added another assignment of my own free will,

To find three things I loved about myself daily until,

Until I knew without a doubt that I was worthy of my own protection,

And I was worthy of a love that offered meaningful connection.

I felt the peace within my soul scream out wanting even more,

Finally knowing that the life I dreamed was in fact possible.

I didn't want a fairytale, I didn't have unrealistic expectations,

I wanted a deeper level of love with emotional intelligence.

Even with this knowledge I was still secure and safe in my solitude,

I know now, it's more important that you give the love you crave back to you.

OVERCOMING ABUSE

*** As previously published in Amazon Best Seller 100 Poems and Possibilities for Healing

They taught me by the tender age of six,

That a girl or woman's ultimate value is sex,

Then again when I was entering my teens at thirteen,

I learned what it was like to freeze under a man of eighteen.

He had a good time, I'm sure he assumed I did too,

But my mind had floated off while my body resumed,

I went home to shower when all was said and done,

Took a razor and cut my face my mind still stunned.

It seemed like the earlier abuse marked me for more,

Like a beacon I didn't know I had calling to its source,

As if somehow they knew I was a damaged easy mark

Because again at seventeen things got infinitely more hard.

I made excuses through all the years about these men,

But a forty year old has no business with seventeen year old children.

Abuse wasn't designated to men that were significantly older in age,

The verbal, physical or sexual abuse was present regardless who I'd date.

They say that if you are the common denominator it's probably you,

So I tried my best to do more healing, to stop future abuse,

And I learned a little more about what not to accept each time,

Still, I found myself having to heal more wounds after each guy.

I was a strong and independent woman, so I shouldn't fall prey to abuse,

Or so everyone seemed to think, along with it won't happen to you,

Obviously, no one would have chosen someone abusive, if we knew,

But our brains are wired chemically to ignore the red flags when its new.

The reality is an abuser rarely shows their true colors in the beginning,

Sometimes the abuse isn't even the result of a bad person scheming,

Sometimes it's incompatibility that isn't realized until you're too far in,

As you both try to be perfect for each other, wanting the relationship to win.

LESSONS FROM AN ABUSED WOMAN

I learned from my mom to be beautiful, make sure you are small,

It seems you are only beautiful if you have no curves at all,

The younger you look, the better your chances will be for love,

But as I grew up, I've learned that's not really love; it's lust.

My mom didn't mean to teach me these lessons,

In truth, it wasn't only her that taught them,

The men in my life reinforced the belief smaller was better,

I was also taught to keep their secrets from her.

Be quiet little girl, just let the men play,

This is just how it is, and this is simply our way,

Afraid of the power a woman could truly harness,

We find any way we can to fold them in darkness

From flat-out abuse, with kicks and fists,

To the subtle manipulation and gaslighting tricks,

Let me dumb this down because you couldn't be smart,

But rest assured, you won't be lovable if you are.

You have to be pretty, and sexy, but not too much,

And only for that one man, but he can have more than one,

And if you are too ambitious, again, you won't be loved,

Because women have no business competing with us.

If you choose to stand on your own two feet alone,

You'll be labeled defective, truth be told,

Because it couldn't possibly be that men have to evolve,

It's the hysterical women that are a problem to be solved.

It's the woman's fault that men are feeling lonely,

By trying to claim their own power or behaving too remotely,

It's the woman's fault that men are feeling less than adequate,

They should have left them to repeat their same old habits.

I DIDN'T TELL HIM

Was I toxic to you he asked, I explained it all away,

You are not toxic but our combination was, I said as the memories replayed.

I told him if he couldn't be emotionally supportive and dated an emotional girl it was toxic,

I told him if I knew I was emotional dated someone who couldn't be supportive it was toxic.

I told him both of these things, so he wouldn't feel attacked,

I put it on my self as well to show that it was just as much my fault we didn't last.

I didn't tell him that I'm terrified to share, or over share, now.

That in social situations I replay the conversations for if they went wrong somehow

I didn't tell him that the times he berated me until I wanted to fade into nothingness

Often lead to times I felt too much and not enough and wanted to cease to exist.

I didn't tell him that I have the most debilitating social anxiety I've ever known

Or that the free spirited girl that would laugh and sing just about anywhere was gone.

I didn't tell him, because it wasn't all his fault,

I had facilitated this relationship too, fighting for it long after I should have walked.

I didn't tell him, because it would have been a target on my back,

As he unleashed a triad of what was wrong with me perceiving all of this as an attack.

I didn't tell him, because it simply wasn't safe too,

I knew if I did he would shift and his words would leave me in despair and doom.

I didn't tell him, because I was conditioned to be good,

Keep everyone happy, mold yourself to their desires, it was understood.

I didn't tell him, that what I needed was to be loved as I am,

Because I thought, in the beginning, that was the kind of relationship we had

I didn't tell him, that toxicity comes from incompatibility,

From trying to force something you know is wrong, ignoring you intuition freely.

I didn't tell him, that it's been 5 years and I'm still scared,

To let anyone see the real me, these wounds are still being repaired.

I didn't tell him, that since him I haven't known another touch,

And while I used to give them out freely I barely allow myself to be hugged.

I didn't tell him, that he was a wound older than his existence in my life,

A challenge from the universe as he tore open old scars for new healing to be applied.

I didn't tell him, that I was gone long before he let me leave,

That I was gone even before I was trapped in the depths of my heaviest grief.

I didn't tell him, that I was trying to build back my self-esteem,

And I knew when I did that, I'd know I deserved more than he would be able to offer me.

I didn't tell him, that he was right when he called me the dark phoenix,

Eventually, all my pain came roaring out, burning everything, and I was finally unleashed from it.

THE MISUSED MAIDEN

Blissfully naive, that is how they saw her,

Unaware it was a defense mechanism cultivated as a child.

Even she was unaware of her naivety, blinded,

Looking at life through rose-colored glasses is misguided.

She felt everything to amazing extremes,

Love, fears, hurt, pain, and all of her dreams.

Overly sensitive and too emotional, they would say,

They didn't know a brain could be simply wired that way.

Searching always to fill this hole she had in her heart,

Not able to be fully herself, always playing a part.

Doing all she could to please as many around her as possible,

Not recognizing this behavior would get her in more trouble.

Believing men when they told her nothing but lies,

Finding out she'd inadvertently been compromised,

She keeps seeking out men who would never be able to provide,

Seeking out partners that would never harmonize.

She couldn't see what she was doing; she thought they needed her love,

She thought everything would be better if she could just love them enough,

This kept her in bad situations longer than you might have thought,

Believing the abuse could be cured, or perhaps goodness taught.

Abuse and misuse do a great deal of damage to the system,

Creating a perpetual cycle and drawing more people twisted,

As they sense the opportunity to take even more from her,

It never even occurred to her that she would be able to dismiss them.

THE HEALING MOTHER

Once the realization of abuse and misuse settled in,

The mother chose to embark on a more serious path of healing.

Becoming a mother meant there was more at stake,

She didn't want her kids to grow up thinking this misuse was okay.

She didn't want her triggers to hit her when she was with her kids,

And she definitely didn't want to be blindsided by it.

Trauma is tricky, and abuse can be more subtle than you think,

It grows roots in the mind and spreads seeds of doubt, insidious.

For a people pleaser, having an external reason to heal was good,

Sure, she did it for herself, but she had to make sure they understood.

Let them see her trying to learn more about healthy relationships,

And if she could, she wanted them to see what real love is.

She might not be able to get out fast enough for them to see,

That a healthy relationship comes with a little more ease,

It's not some massive explosion when someone disagrees,

But this relationship grew into something it wasn't in the beginning.

The constant stress of needing to anticipate his needs,

And being stuck in a relationship that wasn't what it seemed,

Took its toll and added more stress, to an already single parent,

By the time she realized what was happening she was embarrassed.

She didn't even know how they got to this point,

But she did the hard work and slowly began to find her voice,

She started to work out better ways to care for herself,

Doing the work of learning about healthy relationships, she had help.

She went to therapy and did the homework they gave,

Doing the work made her realize she'd have to leave him one day,

When it was all said and done, he had the last word,

But she wanted it that way; it was the outcome she preferred.

Ties were cut, and a deeper and more intensive healing began anew,

She had to heal from her past, and now she had to heal this damage, too,

She had to learn to trust again, and she wasn't sure she should,

Content to live her life alone, it was safer, and she knew she could.

A happiness that seemed elusive, and nearly impossible was tangible again,

As she learned to give herself all the love that she felt she was missing,

And that hole the Maiden desperately kept trying to fill,

She learned how to fill that with self-love as well.

THE RECOVERED CRONE

Through wizened eyes, there is more compassion for one's self,

There is no longer the need to ask for unnecessary help,

No longer the burning desire to fill the black hole within,

With false love, toxicity, or empty promises.

With time you'll come to see the love you were in need of,

Was buried deep within, shrouded within the trauma.

You'll learn to set aside the could've, would've should'ves,

As you heal yourself more deeply and learn self-love.

You'll gain a certain amount of grace, that you give with discretion,

No longer finding it necessary to excuse repeated transgressions.

You no longer seek to be the savior, or make continued excuses,

Like they didn't mean to, or they didn't know they were abusive.

Instead, you find yourself understanding more about compatibility,

And you place more and more emphasis on personal accountability,

Simultaneously, you place more value on simplistic stability.

Recognizing the chaos was only a comfortable liability.

You can look back with compassion on the past life you lead,

And forgive yourself for being naive or flat-out stupid.

You give yourself the grace you eagerly gave the undeserving,

And you finally understand your heart is worth preserving.

There is no bitterness in your heart for the hard lessons taught,

Simply deep introspective and reflective thoughts.

As you've done the hard and tumultuous healing work,

You can finally sit back and enjoy the perks.

The love you give yourself now is so powerful and true,

You know you'll keep yourself safe from that which you outgrew.

All of the trust issues you battled with throughout the years,

They fall away as you learn to trust the person in the mirror.

Overtime the fights begin, accompanied by an erosion of self,

It happens so slowly you remain unaware of the dangers, or need for help.

Like the frog in the pot of water, you can't feel the temperature rise,

Everyone outside can see you cooking, but you think everything is fine.

Perhaps, toxicity comes from trying to force an incompatible match,

And we need not label the person, toxic, abusive, terrible or bad.

While acknowledging they are bad or toxic for us to have the life we deserve,

And moving forward having taking with us everything we have learned.

But, how do we turn off the beacon that was activated when we were young?

How to we tell our brain not to ignore the red flags as we move on?

We have to unlearn a lot of detrimental subconscious lessons taught,

By other broken persons who inflicted that damage without thought.

The journey will be individual to each person that chooses the path,

And healing can be difficult but it's something we a deserve to have,

We won't be robbed of a life of happiness because of others evil deeds,

We will rise from the ashes of our trauma and become all we are meant to be.

Your Misuse Free-Writing:

YOUR MISUSE FREE-WRITING:

Join me in another writing session.

Have you ever felt mistreated, misused, or experienced abuse? Have you witnessed it in others? I invite you to write about your experiences, thoughts, or reflections on your experience or anything that resonated in this chapter.

Your Misuse Poem(s)

YOUR MISUSE POEM(S)

I invite you to read your free writing and look for any poetry in it. Use it as inspiration to write your own "misuse" poems, or just let the poetry flow through you. Sometimes circling words that rhyme can help you see patterns.

Grief

The Echoes of You,
Resonate within my heart,
Grief's last gift to me.

It's another difficult topic because it is uncomfortable and makes others uncomfortable. That seems a little silly to me, considering we all experience loss. It is the one thing we will have in common with each other. We will all lose those that we love. I've learned grief is unique to each person, processing it is not linear, and grief waves can hit anytime. A safe person is someone you can go to without fear, without judgment, who will either ask how to be there for you or know from past exchanges how to be there for you. Some people can't be safe, which is okay, but it is important to find safe people. No one should be left to grieve alone. There are many support groups for various types of loss, and they can be very helpful on your journey. Life coaches, counselors, therapists, and close friends are all potential parts of grief support that you can seek out. One of the most powerful exercises that helped me was a gratitude exercise, where I found three things I was grateful for each day. It seemed impossible initially, but it made a massive positive impact. I found physical activity and walking in nature were also incredibly helpful on my grief journey.

WHO LOVES ME

So, who loves me now,

I cried when you died.

So, who's left me here,

You've left me behind.

So, who's going to care,

There's no one left here,

An angel lost on Earth

Because you left her here.

So, who loves me now,

You've left me all alone,

And you didn't say goodbye,

You just went away to fly.

Who do I trust?

Where do I find love?

So, who loves me now?

Bury me in the ground.

Six feet deep along with you,

I'll close my eyes and be with you,

No one could take care of me but you,

Now that you are gone, what do I do?
Who do I trust?

Where do I find love?

So, who loves me now?

I'm a little white dove.

I'm flying in a direction,

Which I don't know,

Like someone took my eyes,

And turned them to stone.

So, who loves me now,

I cried when you died,

You've left me alone,

And now I want to fly.

LOVE ME

I cannot walk away from your grave,

And leave your soul to dance alone.

I cannot leave your side, without feeling lost inside,

I cannot let you go, without feeling very low.

Tell me a story, say goodbye,

See the tears form in my eyes.

Take me with you; don't hold back,

My life, it seems, is far worse than that.

Love is lost, hearts are broken,

Every Whisper is a token.

Close your eyes, and you will see,

You left me alone, so now, who loves me?

I BLEED

In the sacred silence of my heart, I bleed.

I bleed for you, for those I have lost, you see.

I will always remember your kindness and smile,

And all the time we shared and all the miles.

My heart bleeds from all of this sorrow that I feel,

And my soul keeps searching for the reasons and ways to heal.

I have carried with me this great sadness that grows,

With everyone that I have lost and those I didn't get to know.

Before I know my time is up,

I need to find that undying love.

I LOVE YOU, MY COUSIN, MY SISTER, MY FRIEND

This loss aches deep within my heart,

So very deep that it tears me all apart.

With all of this anger and sadness, I cry,

But these tears can't bring you back to life.

I wish I knew what went through your mind,

I wish that I could turn back time,

I just don't understand why you didn't call me,

Instead, you left me in utter agony.

This pain twists inside my soul

It's dark and painful and won't let go.

It pulls me around and inside out,

And leaves me twisted on the ground.

Without you, life has lost its shine,

Your smile used to light up lives.

Without you, many will be lost,

You used to be the one so strong.

I will miss your charm and smiling face,

Without my heart, there is another empty space.

I love you, my cousin, my sister, my friend,

I will never understand this tragic end.

IT'S NEVER TOO LATE

I hear a song that says, "It's never too late."

Every time I hear this song, I see your face.

It's too late for me to tell you I love you.

Too late, to show you how we all cared.

It's too late for me to fix everything.

Too late for me to make sure I was there.

I wish that I could turn back the hands of time,

To show you how we all thought you shined.

But it's too late to save you from your thoughts,

It's too late to see you drowning in the dark.

Too late for you to see that we saw you shine,

And it's far too late for all of us to make the time.

We all wish we had more time to spend with you,

Never realizing our opportunity would end so soon.

THE SADDEST THING

I can not walk by the lilacs without thinking of you,

I can not think of my future without know that it is true.

It's true that you have left me here without my truest friend,

And it's true that I don't want to feel this darkened loss again.

He can not listen to the music without thinking of you,

He can not give up his dream because of you.

You give him the strength he needs, just to make it through,

And the saddest thing of all was your friendship was true.

She can not walk through the house now without crying to herself,

Your loss weighed heavy on her heart with all of her doubts.

She can not think of all the things should've done together,

Without also thinking of the times you had in stormy weather.

Again, I feel the darken loss as I lost another friend,

And the saddest thing of all is he was true until the end.

We all have lost a loved one, and it's hard to know why.

But we have to continue to believe, and know it's okay to cry.

BROKENHEARTED

Will broken hearts ever mend?

Will happiness meet the end?

Will everything disappear?

Take a look in the mirror.

Who are you, do you know?

What are you looking for, looking for love?

Love's been lost a long, long time,

Suddenly, falling feels like flying.

Dancing feels like floating,

Singing feels like loving,

Everyone's filled with caring,

No one's really boasting.

Time heals all wounds,

I'm left here without you,

Brokenhearted, I still stand,

I continue to fly over the land.

Painful tears so full of rain,

Water falls from the sky of rain,

Memories flood your head,

Memories that have no end.

Broken hearts will never mend,

The world is coming to an end,

It's your heart that will never mend,

There's too much sadness in your head.

MY BABY'S GONE

She offered me whatever I could need,

A ride, something to do, comfort, and stability.

I thought that she would always be there for me,

But the time came, and I made her leave.

I miss my baby, she meant the world to me,

Her sounds, her quirks, and her glistening,

I wish I could have cared for her more,

Maybe then I wouldn't have closed the door.

I wish I had just one more ride,

Just one more day to spend inside,

Just one more day wouldn't be enough,

I wish losing her wasn't this tough.

She listened to me when no one else would,

And made me as comfortable as she could,

I should have cared for her just a little more,

Now, I feel her loss more than ever before.

DEARLY DEPARTED

I hear you call out to me again, but you are not there,

I think back to all of the promises made, empty as the air,

Empty because you never got the chance to follow them through,

Empty because I must now live my life here without you.

In the darkest blackest night, I still hear your voice,

I know somewhere inside of me that death was not your choice,

Still, I feel a bitterness that cries, why didn't you try,

Couldn't you have fought to stay for just a little while?

Why do I feel that I could have stayed the hand of death?

I know it seems irrational, but your voice echoes in my head.

I wondered to myself if I might have lost my mind that night,

There is always one word that resonates within me, why?

So unfair it seems to me to continue to lose the ones I love,

Every year, it seems to me, that I have lost yet another one,

Still, in the darkest corners of my mind, I tell myself not to cry,

I believe that you have found a peace that you could not find in this life

SHATTERED WITH LOSS

I left my heart under the fallen leaves,

I left my soul dancing in sweet misery.

I lost pieces of myself losing you, no one left,

No one to fill that empty place in my life.

You were too young to go, leaving everyone you know.

Three children you left lost without a real home,

One brother who won't call, a sister further lost,

Another whose left standing shrouded in unknown,

I left pieces of myself scatted to the wind with your last breath,

Now, I will struggle to gather them back after all this.

DESPAIR

Sometimes I feel this strange feeling of despair,

It creeps in for no reason until I realize it's there.

Once it takes over, I wish I could dissipate into the air,

To meld into the earth, it would be as if I was never there.

I feel as though life is a movie that someone else is watching,

It's an illusion, and I'm the one that is always and forever or never talking,

I am that character that is replaceable, that no one would really truly miss,

They would say, "What was her name? Oh yeah." and I'd be dismissed

Eventually, the despair will leave, and I will once again feel peace,

I would think about how I felt while it was here and feel I was being silly,

Yet in the back of my mind, in a dark and quiet corner, despair sits,

Smiling its' evil smile, waiting for his next chance to strike another hit.

HEALING FROM LOSS

I remember the day I got that call,

A life was taken, and you were gone.

An empty hole in my heart larger,

One that would make my life harder.

A void that no one else could make better,

It changed me, made me blind and weaker.

I felt everything I loved would be lost forever,

I was fastened to a sinking ship strongly tethered.

Slowly, I began to gather strength once more,

When I realized you remained deep in my core.

You helped me, guided me, and things started to fit,

But still, sometimes, I have the deepest, darkest sadness.

I miss you more than words or tears can express,

Yet I know you would want me to go on and live.

You would want me to dance and sing my heart away,

And so, I will, and I will remember and love you every day.

OKAY TO MOURN

Depression, is that so?

Do you have to put a name to it?

Does it have to be abnormal to mourn?

Pain is not hurt, is it?

The law says no, pain does not matter,

Only broken bones and physical evidence matter.

Money is that everything?

Some would say no, it does not buy happiness,

Others would say how do you know?

Fearless, is that what you say?

I would contend it is normal behavior,

As it is being sad and not afraid to show.

A GROUP, A LOSS

Once, I had a big group of friends,

Who I believed would be there until the end.

I fear this assumption was wrong once again,

And one by one, I lost almost all of those friends.

One was the center, the glue of the group,

The others deferred to him, to know what to do,

Always, I could talk with him, even after the years.

And it seemed as if nothing changed while he lent me his ears.

Slowly, inch by inch the fabric was torn

A friend against friend and a woman scorned

Caught up in the middle without ever a clue

All was breaking down the solid, sticky glue

One day, things got steadily worse for our group,

The heart and soul of our friends decided to move,

And then another and yet another moved away with him too,

That is the way of things, people are there to lose.

I was forgotten of, spurned, written off, or of no use,

But I still knew in my heart that I was left with a few,

A few friends from the world up north, who I thought I knew.

Nothing like my friends back home, but still friends I thought were true.

One day, when the waters were calm, death struck again,

She took one of the calmest, rational, and kindest of friends.

It hardly seemed fair to bring his life to an end,

He was thoughtful and kind and missed by every one of his friends.

Rollercoaster rides of emotions finally subsided to a straightaway,

One friend emerged stronger than before, connected in an ethereal way.

Still, the losses we have felt left us empty and betrayed,

It seems to me that life can be a cruel and depressing masquerade.

SURVIVE

In the deepest, darkest, most consuming despair,

I have faltered and wished I were not here.

They say you must reach the bottom before the top,

I have reached it a few times now, and I'm ready to go up.

I made the decision after the despair was less consuming.

I decided I would make a promise to those who knew me,

In the deepest, darkest, and most desperate of times,

Never need you to wonder if I would ever take my life.

I have seen the pain taking a life has wrought,

I have felt the anguish of many that were lost.

Too well I understand what in that moment is felt,

I know how consuming the pain is locked within yourself.

But I also know that you have to learn how to let go.

Let go of the hurts, and don't be afraid to let someone know.

The answers to all of your questions lay within yourself.

They might be hard to find, but you will find them with some help.

So, in your deepest darkest, most consuming despair.

When you feel like there is no one that will truly be there.

In the deepest darkest and most desperate of times.

Never forget the pain and anguish for others if you took your life.

RIVER OF TEARS TO HEAL

In the deepest despair I had ever known,

I was lost beyond measure.

Bereft in a fog so deep I couldn't see

Drowning in tears that created the river.

The river that could have drowned me,

Stealing away my life.

Yet, instead, the river was my ally,

Carrying me away from the darkness to the light.

The river, created of the deepest pain and anguish,

Born of my own grief.

Was the very river I would ride,

Not knowing it was born of and carrying me to release.

From the darkest days that seemed never-ending,

To the fog that wouldn't clear.

It seemed impossible to believe.

That I would find the light again the next year.

But the water can be relentless that way,

Holding memories in its drops.

It remembered who I was,

My tears held memories even when I was lost.

I owe that river a great debt of gratitude,

To have brought me home.

It has done the impossible,

The tears allowed me to heal, and to move forward once more.

TRANSITION

The darkness seemed so dense,

I didn't believe there was a way out of this.

All my light seemed starved away,

And I thought I wouldn't smile another day.

All my laughter and joy locked up tight,

Gone forever, I thought, like my own light,

Doomed, I felt, to wander in darkness and grief,

Likely, for all of eternity.

Yet, I didn't give up as completely as I thought,

And though it seemed impossible, I still fought.

I fought to find some sliver of light and some peace,

If happiness wasn't an option, perhaps, peace was for me.

It still seemed impossible that I might find myself,

And the truth is I was forever changed into someone else.

But as I took the advice and wisdom from counsel, I sought,

The slightest sliver of light was cast to me to be caught.

Like a fishing line barely visible but there I reached out,

Despite my grief, my fears, my guilt, and all my doubt.

I held that delicate line, afraid and ashamed of the hope,

Could I really move forward? Could I learn healthy ways to cope?

I kept working on the arduous work of healing,

Working towards happiness but not really believing.

Anyone who tells you therapy is easy might be wrong,

But it is worth working on even if the process is long.

There were days I wanted to give up, but I pressed on,

One day, without warning, the darkness was a less oppressive fog.

Instead of blackness and darkness consuming me whole,

I was in greys and shadows, but there was light to behold.

Suddenly, there were paths before me to choose from,

I knew I was forever changed, but I could smile some.

I kept walking forward through the fog, intent on healing,

And eventually, happiness, joy, and peace were possible and appealing.

Now I know when I get lost in the darkest of dark,

That it isn't forever, and the darkness will part,

Giving way to the light even if I cannot see it at the time,

Now, I know if I put in the work and believe in myself, I'll once again rise.

I PRAY OR WISH

I pray you never know depression,

But if you do, I pray you always have hope,

And if you find yourself losing hope

I pray you remember that choosing to end your life will transfer your pain to everyone you love,

And that their life will be made worse and not better by your loss,

Those you love will be riddled with doubts, what-ifs, guilt and darker thoughts,

And if you can't believe that I pray you think about the person who will find you because they will be traumatized,

They will live with fear, nightmares, and indescribable pain, horrified.

Plagued by the images of a decision made by yourself,

And if you still can't find hope or some glimmer of light, I pray you get help,

And if you can't or won't, I pray for your loved ones Mental Health,

Because no one should know this pain, it's hell.

UNTHINKABLE

You did the unthinkable, but was it,

It wasn't unthinkable if you thought it,

You made a decision to shatter our worlds,

To make every aspect of my life worse.

They tell me I'll heal, but the truth is I won't.

A part of me died with you, everyone knows.

So, I grieve for you, the decision you made,

The loss of our home that you threw away.

The loss of who I once was before this,

And I hate this selfish act that you believed to be selfless.

I look for you in the rearview mirror,

To ask you questions as you look to your sister.

I look for you everywhere I go, because you were always there.

Which means my grief is just as heavy everywhere.

It'll be eight months since I found you in your room,

Staring into nothingness in shock that there was nothing I could do.

Screaming and crying, in shock and denial equally,

I wished and prayed that I'd wake up from this horrific dream.

I didn't wake up, and no answers were ever revealed.

All of us wondering when and why this solution appealed.

Leaving those who survived in the wake of your earth-shattering decision,

To try and pick up the pieces with much indecision.

The aftermath of your choices echoes through our lives,

Each of us now has all we can do to desperately try and survive.

Forever, we will be changed by your actions.

Lost, broken, incomplete, and in desperate need of compassion.

BLACK HOLE HEART

Everyone's world keeps turning while mine stays still,

They are all moving on, but I'm stuck here in limbo with you.

They keep smiling and dancing, buying new toys and finding love,

But I'm stuck with this black hole in my heart and no air in my lungs.

A TREE

I'm not upset about the choice we made,

To turn you into a tree seemed right that day.

You loved climbing trees, said they helped you think,

Drew me a picture of Groot, I didn't see the interlink.

I wish I knew your mind had grown darker than night,

like a deep forest so thick it shuts out the light.

You were just a sapling, not yet grown to potential,

Perhaps feeling like a burden, even though you were essential.

As we planted you, doubt struck me, with tremendous force.

Was there anything I could have done to change your course?

I used to seek the solitude and peace of the woods often,

With each visit I'd hoped the emotions roiling within would soften.

How I wished I could find that solitude and peace those days,

Now instead I find myself more often wandering in a daze.

My world completely shattered by your decision to end your life,

That all the greenery, leaves and branches can't alleviate my strife.

All I can do now is visit and hope your roots grow strong,

And hope that you finally found a place you belong.

I chose to believe as you grow into that mighty tree,

With each extension, each new leaf you find more peace.

DAGDA

My beautiful striped, orange cat,

You were with me longer than any parent,

You spent more time with me than any other human,

And your loss broke my heart into fragments.

The unconditional love I got to experience with you,

As you perched on my shoulder purring,

Always sensing when I needed help getting through,

You knew when I was sad, stressed, or hurting.

I suppose most other people wouldn't understand,

The grief I experienced as you reached your paw to my hand,

Howling in pain as the I told you it was okay,

If you were ready to leave me to stop the pain.

I grieved heavily for many days and many weeks,

Society looked upon me as if I were weak,

Cruel to those who have lost their furry friends,

Asking us when will I, just get over it.

If you have had a beloved cross the rainbow bridge,

You know the pain, the grief, and how it hits,

You also know you would not have done it differently,

Every bit of time spent was worth the commitment.

ZOE

Her beautiful face lay gently in my lap,

Her big brown eyes looking up at me,

It was as if she felt my pain instantly,

Asking nothing in return, she sat with me and my grief.

AFTER THIS LIFE

Though the light streamed down on you, you did not grow,

Perhaps it was because you were in the woods alone,

Maybe the earth felt to foreign for you to rest,

Or perhaps you missed the times I would tuck you in to bed.

Perhaps your memories found their way in through the roots,

And you simply didn't know what you should do,

Or you remembered climbing trees at our old home,

And wished that you had chosen to go down a different road.

Whatever the reason I couldn't leave you there in the dark,

Down in the soil away from all our loving hearts,

So I dug you back up with a small shovel and my hands,

And we brought you home so you could become a tree instead

And when we finally setting down and fine our new home,

I will take great joy in planting you there to continue to grow,

And I'll get to share you with all those that loved you so,

And perhaps, having you there our home will really feel like home.

LEARNING GRIEF

*** As previously published in Amazon Best Seller 100 Poems and Possibilities for Healing }

Society can be cruel to the grieving heart,

They say get over it before the healing can start,

And so many people busy their grief away,

I was one of them until the most tragic of days.

My grief journey started when I was eleven years old,

It probably started before then, but that's how memory goes,

My dear nana and papa fell ill around the same time,

And though we did everything we could we couldn't stop the tide.

I was a bit too young to understand all the emotions that I felt,

And again I seemed to struggle with grief when my dad left,

But society doesn't give us time and space to really breath,

And it doesn't consider all the different types of grief.

So I just buried the feelings deep down inside,

And when, at thirteen, my mom sent me away I just cried

Later when the anger surfaced I didn't think it was grief,

Because, handling grief wasn't something anyone taught me.

At fifteen when she died of the plague we call cancer,

The swirl of emotions was destined to lead me to disaster.

Still, I had no real valuable grief education to lean upon

So I floundered about trying everything and anything to move on

When my grandmother died her words echoed through my mind,

Think positive and positive things will happen, I felt purpose stir inside,

I coped with her death by starting my very own experiment,

I would honor her by testing the words that became my inheritance.

It seemed to me every couple years yet another person died,

And I continued to busy away my grief convinced I was fine.

One day we lost my precious cousin, a teen, to suicide,

I found even more things to busy my schedule and pass the time.

The grief still found it's way in as I found the four agreements,

A book that seemed to save me from my state of bereavement.

I embarked on another phase of my journey, shifting my mind

I leaned more heavily into healing as I busied away more time.

I thought I was a pro, there was no loss that would make me backslide

Until the most tragic of days, I lost my own teen child to suicide.

Despite all my research and healing nothing prepared for this time,

I felt like the darkness would consume me forever and I'd forever lost my light.

I didn't just loss my child that day, I lost so much more

This grief was heavier and deeper than anything I'd experienced before

I sold my home because I couldn't go back to the place he died,

I lost my sense of security, I lost my own internal flame burning inside.

Out of my greatest darkness, grief and despair came a deeper understanding,

With intentional choice, hard work on healing I felt my knowledge expanding,

Suddenly, I realized I never really learned how to process my grief fully

I learned it came in waves, and that society would be my greatest bully.

Everyone will experience their grief journey uniquely and at their own pace,

And a safe person was someone that would be there holding safe space,

When the grief burst hit it's okay for you to sit with or lean into the waves

They won't last forever, but I do remember them lasting for days.

I hate the saying that "it gets easier with time" that seemed like a lie,

But you get stronger as you add more tools to your tool belt that you can apply,

When you think your flame is gone, just feed it the healing spark to ignite

And that internal flame that we all have, is eternal, it will always be inside.

TRANSFORMED

*** As previously published in Amazon Best Seller 100 Poems and Possibilities for Healing

I thought, I can't survive this...

How could I? It's too horrendous.

The loss of a child, seeing him lifeless,

There is no possible way I can survive this.

All the light I was made up of had gone dark.

My flame, my inner light, extinguished, gone.

I'll never smile or laugh, or feel joy again.

How could I ever feel any of that after losing him.

Someone told me, a few months after,

Happiness is a choice, Your happiness matters,

But I didn't choose this, I rebelled against the thought.

He chose this and the world as I know it is gone.

But I continued my path, trying to heal for her,

She still needed a parent, more than ever, I was sure,

Healing was hard, and I was told more than once,

Life is for the living, and that I deserved love.

Assigned a gratitude assignment I baulked,

I found it hard to be grateful for anything at all.

I'd have given him my last breath after all,

I couldn't even be grateful for breathing, so I started small.

I was grateful for my girl, my pets and my experience being mindful,

I was grateful that I still found the sun, the moon and stars tranquil,

Some days I was grateful a stranger smiled, or said something hopeful,

For my resilience, my healing, and my compassion, I was grateful.

I didn't think this assignment would do much for me at the time,

But I was dedicated to it, and perhaps the assigner was right.

I used to do this regularly, but it was harder to see the gratitude this time,

Still the more I looked for things to be grateful for the more I could find.

Suddenly, it was there, that flicker of light inside.

I had to continue my healing, I had to give it a try,

Was it possible that the flame inside hadn't truly died?

Was it possible, that this was something I could survive?

By the third year I could smile and even laugh once more,

It was clear that I couldn't simply be who I was before,

And though I was still on a journey to find my new norm,

I had survived once again, but I wasn't the same, I was transformed.

A LEGACY OF KINDNESS AND GRATITUDE

You didn't believe in half or step,

You only believed in whole,

And every child remotely connected,

Became a child of your own.

Through all that you endured,

You maintained a heart of gold,

You didn't become distant,

Or bitter, or cold.

I'll forever recount the stories,

Of your tiny little fists,

Bringing to our dad,

A little swift justice,

I'll remember all the times,

You held me as a child

And sang to me sweet lullabies,

Doing your best to make me smile.

And how you loved the children,

Of two different women,

As they were your own,

With little or no difference.

See there is something to be said,

About a woman of your caliber,

Something to aspire to,

That most never chase after.

Your kindness leaves a legacy,

A way to honor you in your absence,

To keep you close within our hearts,

We practice kindness until it's a habit.

Expressing gratitude for all you were,

Is yet one other way,

To honor your memory and spirit,

We seek to be grateful for every day.

And though we know that grief is hard,

And it will hit us in waves,

We will sit with our memories of you,

Thankful for all of those moments and days.

Every single one of us,

That mourn you here today,

Will shed our tears of joy,

When we meet again someday.

MOM

We all expect to lose our parents one day,

And yet, when we do, the grief still comes in waves.

It doesn't matter if we lose them young or old,

Our grief is heavy and if you know you know.

I will always wish I could pick up the phone and call,

Whenever there is news to share big or small.

I will always feel your absence when we celebrate life,

Feeling at least a little as if, for me, something was denied.

I will still feel like you were taken from me far too soon,

And my grief will be present like a never-ending wound.

Some days I will smile as the memories come in floods,

And other days I will sob over the many memories of us.

As a parent, I will grieve, when I learn lessons from my own kids,

And I lament that many people take for granted this privilege.

For, it was indeed a privilege to have you as my mother,

And I feel like I didn't tell you enough how much I love you.

I'm grateful for every lesson that I learned because of you,

From the really big life lessons to teaching me to tie my shoes.

The empty space in my heart from your loss will never be filled,

And my grief will be present because my love for you will never yield.

THE GRIEVING MAIDEN

Hit with grief too young,

Uncertain what it all means,

Believing for a time, it could be undone,

She coped by keeping busy.

A cruel and harsh society,

Telling her everyone's replaceable,

And if she must grieve, do it quietly,

Drawing attention to her pain was unacceptable.

They told her grief was not conversational,

You'll make others uncomfortable.

If she did talk, she was labeled sensational,

Sometimes, they are even called insufferable.

As she lost others like dominos,

Grief seemed increasingly inescapable.

With each loss, it was like a sinkhole,

Yet, she found herself unbreakable.

She knew the truth, they were irreplaceable,

Thinking otherwise came at a high cost.

The funny thing about grief is it is situational,

It hits you differently for each person lost.

She may have been too young to lose so many,

And when she'd see others with a mother,

She sometimes got hit with loss and envy,

As she accepted, some waves were just tougher.

They never told her it was okay she wasn't okay,

It was quite the opposite,

Society just didn't work that way.

She was expected to quickly get over it.

Grief wasn't about the person experiencing it,

It was about everybody else.

And it created an inner conflict,

For anyone who wanted to help.

Even for her, who lost so much,

Desperately wanting others to know,

This was something they could overcome,

And grief leaves no one untouched.

She would break away from the societal norms,

Seeking help for her state of mind

Focusing on her emotional growth

As she busied away much time.

Busyness became her greatest coping mechanism,

As she found more and more to occupy her mind.

She found her increasing perfectionism,

Another side effect of grief declined.

Burying her face in self-help books,

Trying to find the answers,

She ignored all the funny looks,

From a society that thought grief could be canceled.

THE GRIEVING MOTHER

The absolutely worst grief she knew,

Was the loss of a child,

And all the busyness in the world,

Wasn't going to make her smile.

In fact, she believed this was the end,

Despite her experience with grief,

She thought she'd never feel happiness again,

And that thought turned into a belief.

She had recovered from every loss,

Up until this one,

Or so she had thought,

In reality, she had only run.

But this one was different,

She couldn't run away.

This loss was the second loss deliberate,

All her techniques were betrayed.

Initially, she didn't want to face it,

Stuck in the stage of avoidance,

Then voraciously reading, trying to shift,

Failing at each deployment.

They put her on medication,

That stole away her memory,

The goal was emotional regulation,

But this wouldn't provide a true remedy.

She would go back to sleep in denial,

Her heart was in constant devastation,

While the mind attempted survival,

Brought her images in preparation.

She would dream of alternate realities,

Trying to find an explanation,

And a plan to avoid this tragedy,

So they could wake up in a safe haven.

Some around her drove her to isolation,

Once again confronted with society,

And their victimizing the victim,

To avoid their own frustration.

Trying to understand the incomprehensible,

And trying to get more education,

She was shocked that valuable information was inaccessible,

Appalled to find the lack of shared information.

Once again, she was confronted,

By societal expectations,

That she does as instructed,

And stifle any communication.

Grief was bad enough, but suicide?

That should never be a conversation,

That was definitely something to hide,

Lest knowledge of it breed consideration.

Society doesn't want true transformation,

That would mean acknowledging mental health,

And after all, it affects the whole population,

Which is just too difficult for them to help.

She saw firsthand the immediate complications,

So many had been told it was normal,

And society likes to keep its separation,

So, if you seek help, you're labeled abnormal.

This just gave her more inspiration,

As she decided to share her stories,

To help others who might experience this situation,

Offering her own unique expertise.

Refusing to bow to society,

Having come out the other side of grief,

No longer suffering silently,

She found a voice to speak.

THE GRIEVING CRONE

When you learn your grief doesn't need outside validation,

You will be freed from grief in your own way,

Which provides you with an amazing liberation.

It really isn't any of your business, others interpretation,

When it comes to your grief,

You need not have any reservations.

You can't avoid or busy away your grief

The waves will hit you harder, so,

Learn to sit with the waves to find release.

I know it can be easy to feel crazy; that's the organization,

That told you this was abnormal,

All the while driving you into desperation.

When I stepped out of my grief into observation,

I saw that our society,

Drove those who were grieving into isolation.

Society, condemning their need for communication,

To share stories of their loved ones,

So, they could honor them in subtle celebration.

Sometimes others who don't understand feel a separation,

They want to be there for you,

But they don't have the tools for practical application.

Another enemy of grief can be the imagination,

It can fool you into believing in,

A false and harmful representation.

Your grief and what you need require investigation,

You deserve a safe person,

But you may have to tell them your needs and expectations.

Healing is very hard and requires dedication,

But you can come out the other side,

With a little determination.

There will be days when you lack all motivation,

And you will question if you will ever,

Feel the once-familiar inspiration.

I can tell you that you will if it's what you desire,

It will be your mindset that will determine,

Your future and that which you will acquire.

I have learned my assets and detriments can be hesitation,

It can help me pause, true,

But it can also stifle my participation.

Without actively participating in my life,

I wasn't really living,

And I knew intuitively that wasn't the design.

So, I knew I had to learn more about grieving,

To give myself a chance,

Truly doing deep and meaningful healing.

I took everything I learned and learned more,

I used everything in my toolbox,

The goal was simple: I would be restored.

There were so many lessons and revelations along the way,

But the message of the grieving crone is,

You can heal; you can start today.

Your Grief Free-Writing:

YOUR GRIEF FREE-WRITING:

I invite you to join me in a free writing session.

Have you ever experienced a loss? Grief is actually a normal part of life. It is with us every day. We can experience grief when we change jobs or when we move, lose a pet, or lose a loved one. We may even experience grief when we lose a car, hand off a project, or lose an item. Have you experienced grief? Have you known someone who has? I invite you to do a bit of free writing, be uncensored, and write freely.

Your Grief Poem(s)

YOUR GRIEF POEM(S)

I invite you to read your free writing and look for any poetry in it. Use it as inspiration to write your own grief poems, or just let the poetry flow through you. Sometimes circling words that rhyme can help you see patterns.

Fighting the Darkness

Trauma is confused,
with other diagnosis,
Prolonging healing.

I know this makes three difficult topics, talking about depression, trauma and suicide is not comfortable, but if we don't talk about it, share our feelings about it, how can we change the alarmingly growing rates of loss to them. Suicide remains a top 10 leading cause of death for most age brackets. I have lost several people to suicide including two teens in my family. I myself attempted suicide as a teen and I know many others that had unsuccessful attempts and I am grateful they failed. I have known many more that struggled with depression, trauma, anxiety or other related mental health issues. Let's normalize sharing these feelings so, they don't fester and grow in the darkness where they thrive. Let's shine a light on them and stop them from growing. In these darker times it can be easy to believe that people will be better of with out, but I can tell you with certainly that they will not. You matter to more people than you realize. I'm glad you are still here.

UNTITLED

Like the brilliant and powerful sun light.

Like the healing moon that shines at night.

It's here it's gone love's disappeared,

External sources shouldn't have been revered.

In this world there is no mercy,

In this world beauty's lost in boundaries.

No more love, it's lost it's light.

This world is becoming as dark as night.

If you're different, you're a freak,

If you're the same, you're weak.

Happiness never last for long, it comes and goes,

As capricious as the wind deciding which way to blow.

Will it ever end, will happiness be in the end?

Before I break, how far can I bend?

Violence had taken over, evil is rising.

Good will prevail, if it has the right timing.

Fate, Faith Lies and betrayal, everything is connected.

Can good live without evil, if it were dissected?

Sadness has taken over, yet, in your soul you wish to be happy,

Take charge, decide, have faith in yourself and make yourself happy.

DARKNESS

It's insidious, the darkness, how it twists its way through your soul and heart.

. . .

It stops you, tortures you, and you will soon find you're tearing yourself apart.

It wants to destroy you, to take you over,

it wants you to be defeated and give up your life.

It wants you to believe you are broken beyond repair,

it wants you to feel despair.

It wants to take away your hope, the idea of love,

everything you cherish.

THE ACCIDENT

Why do I sit here filled with rage?

Where did it come from, did it come from age,

Why, since the accident can't I calm down.

I sit here trying to figure all this out,

Even through my headaches, and of them I've had many,

I have never felt anger over anything so petty.

Sometimes I'm not sure why I'm even mad,

And thinking of those questions, makes me feel sad.

One day I was okay and the next I was on pills,

As if the pills could cure all my ills.

I think it funny sometimes, how I lost everything.

Once when I lost my mom, and again when I lost my being,

I thought that no one could take away who you were,

But I find I was mistaken, again, about this cruel world,

I think of nature to be kind and lend me her hand,

But sometimes she is not there, and my feet burn on the sand,

I wish to the heavens that I was not in so much pain,

And that my struggle to keep going is not in vain.

I hope every day that I will have the strength,

To continue through life never knowing which way.

STRESS

Goodbye to the world of cruelty,

I have had enough, not me.

Hurt beyond the point of return,

I will continue to yearn.

I long for a happiness long forgotten,

And find that life as lost it's volume.

I need so much more than I imagined,

I wonder if it's worth fight for, can I be happy?

I miss you mom, and I've tried hard to continue,

But I'm not sure I'll make it through.

Strong as I am, I'm getting nowhere, and stress continues

To add to the pile of things, unnecessary, but there,

I miss you, I have no one to talk to right now,

So I write, I suppose in that way, you're always there.

OKAY TO CRY

Alone in a world where only the strong survive,

I try to be as strong as anyone inside,

Depression and illness are not an option,

But still sometimes it's okay to cry.

LIFE ALONE

Alone I sit.

Alone I breathe.

Alone I think.

Alone I see.

Life is hard.

Life is not fair.

Life is painful.

Life is hard to bear.

SADNESS

Far away, far behind,

No one seems to be that kind.

· · ·

Sweet, serene, silent screams,

No more love for a precious dove.

Lost all respect, lost all hope,

Lost all morals, unable to cope.

Sweet, sweet sadness, involves a lot of madness,

As you're left alone, to protect your own.

Feeling down, doesn't go away,

You're left with this feeling, every single day.

No one seems to care, no one seems aware,

Of this sadness inside, that only you can prepare.

HAPPY I'M GONE?

Tomorrow may not come,

Would you have told me all your love?

If tomorrow never came,

Would you regret anything?

When tomorrow never comes

Will you be happy that I'm gone?

GHOSTS FROM MY PAST

I am left alone with the ghosts from my past,

To sit and write how I feel so very sad.

Alone, left without any one to comfort me,

I struggle to rid myself of this inner misery.

So sad are my writings everyone says,

But never will they understand the thoughts in my head.

I have tried so very hard to be as happy as you,

But things I have been through, you never knew.

You left, he left, she left me alone,

And no one wants to see me or use the phone.

Over emotional left behind too many die,

Leave me then if you want, I say goodbye.

Lost, abandoned, lonely afraid,

You'll keep hurting me this way.

It's a shame it's so unintentional,

Yet still it hurts no less at all.

I must overcome these feelings I have,

But I must do it alone, on my own path.

No one wants to deal with me or help me out,

So, I have to find a way to figure this out.

No one, alone, in solitude I sit,

My mind is churning a mile a minute.

Surrounded my complacency and death,

Change was never to by my friend.

Lost so very, very lost I cry,

Why isn't someone here with me tonight.

I suppose I brought this on myself,

I should have known no one would help.

It's all just me and my over sensitivity,

But I've talked to many that understand me.

Well not me but my particular issues,

But then it is them who matters, not me, so what can I do.

FIGHTING DOUBT

Riddled with self-doubt,

Standing on the ledge of indecision,

Perhaps I should give in,

Let the doubt defeat me, at least it's a decision.

Would it bring me peace of mind,

To just walk away form it all,

To just toss all my dreams aside,

Would I then feel as though I stopped my fall.

For falling I am, into despair,

Grasping at the roots of the trees.

As the night and darkness cling to me,

Will I stop or will I know defeat.

. . .

I am a survivor, that I know for sure,

With many nights of sorrow and terror.

These challenges continue to haunt me, a love,

That promises fairy tales and horrors no more.

FEAR

It strangles me this fear inside,

What is happening to me, who am I?

I was never the one to run away,

Never would I live my life afraid?

It suffocates me this fear that I have,

It won't let me go, am I going mad?

I can't seem to get rid of it as hard as I try,

I just want to let go and let myself cry.

It closes all around me this darkness,

It squeezes me into that nothingness,

I'm so afraid to be hurt and to fail,

But I have to try and get out of this jail.

I am captive to these dark feelings inside,

I have no one to comfort me while I cry.

Where is that fairy tale I once dreamed of,

Where is the knight to give me his love.

It wraps around me, and it will not let go,

I fight with it I struggle, where did you go?

I find no comfort at all in this blackest of holes,

And without you into the nothingness I go.

I fall spiraling into the chaos out of control,

Your arms reach out to me, and you grab hold.

Your voice whispers to me "I will not let go."

And I just hope that to your promise you will hold.

LOST DREAMS

Fairytales are legends and dreams,

Some are destined to come true,

While others die hard at your feet.

Dreams come true if you make them,

Some things in life we control,

But matters of emotions are left to fate.

No one controls the destiny of love,

And your fairytale may simply be a dream,

But you choose a hat to look at it.

You may see the glass half full,

While I see it too often half empty.

And my tears do not fill it much more.

SILENT WORDS

Sometimes the silent words of a lover's mouth,

Are the words that echo louder than any sound.

And in the silence of a lonely night,

Your memory probes the last silent fight.

Quiet and fierce is the lover's heart,

Wronged and alone and set far apart.

The lover remembers the words unspoken,

And pounds gentle hands into nothing.

The air sweeps around the pounding fists,

And tries to offer silent soothing gentleness.

Deep inside the hurt does not stop,

But seems to move slowly to one single spot.

The heart is full of love and hurt.

It cries out loud as if being murdered.

Silent no more the heart cannot bear it.

The heart is shattering into thousands of fragments.

Now the silence sweeps across the land,

It finds the murderer and it then forms a hand.

Squeezing his heart, he will feel her pain too,

As the silent words spoken are now silenced too.

WHAT A WORLD THIS IS

What a world this is that confuses me,

That does not let me be me.

What a world this is that breaks my heart,

It leaves me alone and apart.

FALLING APART

She had everything, everything that she set out for.

She had a home, a home that she worked so hard for.

She had great friends that thought the world of her.

She found a job so she could rely only on her.

But that dark despair keeps covering her heart.

And though everything seems fine she's falling apart,

And she cries at night sometimes hoping it's her last,

Then she fights the darkness hoping it will pass.

She fought hard and challenged all of her past.

She forgave the wrongs and forgave herself at last.

She found herself finally growing strong.

She commits to herself to laugh every day.

VANISH

Sometimes I wish I could just vanish from sight,

I could escape to another world filled with beautiful moonlight.

Sometimes I wish I could fly somewhere new,

I could escape from the thoughts and feelings of you.

I've tried to let go but the memories stay so strong,

I've tried to move on, but I'm singing the same song.

I can't seem to break this vicious cycle I am in.

I'm trapped in this world so full of hurt, hate and sin.

STUCK IN DEPRESSION/DEFECTIVE DOLL

What do you do when you want to sleep forever?

Not die exactly but stay in a peaceful slumber,

It's true they say you hurt the ones you love the most,

Because I have been hurt and always by the ones I love.

What do you do with constant nagging disappointment?

Expectations lead to failure so what is the point of it?

It is true, sometimes, I even expect too much from myself,

Maybe I am the defective doll on the conveyor belt.

What do you do when you think you have nothing left to give?

Constantly trying to make everyone happy until it sinks in.

They're not trying to make you happy; this is a one-way road.

It's too bad you're on a dead-end street about to lose control.

· · ·

What do you do when all your dreams fade away to obscurity?

You realize that your dreams are never meant to be reality.

No one can help you preserve something that's already gone,

You're stuck in the life you lead with the road ahead too long.

What do you do when you just can't think about what is going on?

Not that you want to leave this beautiful earth for very long,

Nature is your refuge and even she can be so cruel,

Yet it is so nice on a beautiful spring day next to a pool.

What do you do when you reach the end of your sanity?

Though, it seems, at this time in life you never thought more clearly,

You try to reason and think about all the good things going on,

But you are a fool and can't help but wait for the next thing to go wrong.

LET IT RAIN

Let it rain,

Let the tears come as they may.

Let it rain,

I'll see you again one day.

Let it rain,

I'm gonna make it through this pain.

Let it rain,

I'll let the tears fall as they may.

THE HERDER

Pain closes around me,

It's claw wrenches deep within,

I scream silently,

No one hears me in the end.

I've carried burdens many times,

Sometimes too many, too big to hold,

So much that I must cry,

And resolve them all on my own.

I carry the world if it falls,

But the world leaves me alone,

Lost inside my solitude I call,

But no one answers, no one's home.

Lost I am, I think forever,

To this depression growing further,

I turn to see what's the matter,

To find that I am the herder.

BITTER TASTE

Sleep doesn't come easy; I am exiled by my own will.

Trapped deep within myself, I continue to fight this battle.

I withdraw further into the darkness the darkness in my mind,

Trying to find some semblance of peace to hide,

Aggression was never a good taste for my heart.

Though it now burns with jealousy and tears me apart,

Longing for the dream that I had for so very long.

My despair has deepened into a frightfully sad song.

SILENT, SECRET, QUIET

Silent are my screams,

That speaks of heartache.

Silent are the prayers,

That I dare to make.

Quiet are the whispers,

That I speak to myself.

Quiet are the secrets,

That is deep inside my heart.

Silenced are the echoes,

That tells my story bold.

Silenced are the sparrows,

That helped me through it all.

Secret are the scars,

Left behind by heartache.

Secret is the pain,

That my love truly makes.

Silent are the birds,

On this saddest of days.

Silent are the trees,

That hides the sun's rays.

Quiet am I now,

Left all alone, by myself.

Quiet am I now,

Hurting inside and out.

HUNGRY SADNESS

Sadness is a feeling, or is it really there,

The thought and sounds of sadness, are not very rare,

It's deadly and its pain, it's something for every day,

It's steely and hungry and feeds on me in every way.

Sadness won't just go away, it squeezes harder and harder,

And just when you feel you can't take it, it stops,

It stops for a second, and then it starts again,

Making sure you must deal with it, and you have to stay.

IT ALL FELL APART

I sat to watch the sun rise,

Only to see it fall.

I gave you a chance to see us together,

Only to see us apart.

I gave my heart away to be filled with love,

Only for you to run.

I gave myself to you to feel happiness,

Only to feel numb.

I gave my all, in this, to make it work,

Only to be left and hurt.

I gave you every reason to stay,

Only for you to go play.

I sat to watch the moon rise,

Only to see no love in your eyes.

I talked to you about it so long,

Only to find you are already gone.

CHOOSE TO LIVE

Life is cruel, hurtful, and deceitful.

Do I lay down and die or push steadily forward?

The hurt within my heart causes me to almost let go.

To find a love that will either heal me or hurt me more.

Torn between worlds and the words I write,

Too keep me from falling into the darkest of nights,

I fight to stay alive when half of me wants to die.

And in my solitude to myself I lie.

I tell myself everything will be alright,

In the downward spiral known as my life,

Everything seems like a lie designed to hurt,

The pain seems suspended only by writing words.

People are cruel even when intentions are good,

Somehow, I still end up more tired and hurt.

I crave a time when I am free of this pain.

When tears don't fall from my eyes like rain.

Two worlds collide and I must choose only one,

But I don't remember having a choice, who won.

I cry, and I scream feeling so utterly abandoned and alone,

As I think to myself do I have, and if so, where is my home?

What am I doing, where have I been.

Why can't I let these things out of my head.

I want to let go of the pain deep inside

But if I let go, what will I leave behind?

DEPRESSION

I'm slipping further and further into a deep and dark pit,

Unable to climb out, it seeks to stop all feelings, except for it.

I fall forever there seems to be no end,

There is nothing to hold onto as I fall further in.

At first, I welcomed it, this darkness around me.

It seemed comforting, in its sleepy surroundings.

Then I tried to fight and clawed and scratched at it,

But there was nothing to hold onto in the cold, dark black pit.

All my sound was swallowed before others heard,

And it was clear to me that no one heard a word.

Before I knew it, I was lost and alone in this feeling,

I knew I had to get myself out, but my reason was failing.

I had to talk to someone and tell them how I felt,

But this feeling controlled me and away the words would melt.

Still, I looked inside, and I knew what I must do,

I had to write a poem about this feeling, in case you felt it too.

LONELY

I am standing at the edge of my sanity,

Nothing holds me or sees that I am safe,

There is no-one here, and no-one is coming to rescue me,

I want out of this world of pettiness and hate.

I dance with death tonight, just like the last,

He holds me then spins me away, so I take flight,

At some point I know he will decide to keep me,

Though now he leaves me here my time is not tonight.

The hatred and fear, the sadness and pain won't leave.

I wish that I had that love that still evades me,

I hold on to the hope that perhaps there is someone for me,

And in my darkest hours I believe in that need.

Yet still I am on the edge of a cliff with no end,

About to give myself away to the darkness once again,

The stress of this world and what it deems important,

Are simply too much for my mind to understand.

The two paths that show themselves quickly disappear.

And I'm left with nowhere to go, and I can't stay here,

So where do I fit in, left alone within myself,

Destined to have no-one left, there is no one that can help.

SURVIVE THE DEPRESSION

I feel a pain deep within my chest,

It doesn't seem to leave, but it's also not constant,

I feel angry, and tire, and lonely,

I wish that I had a reason, but it is just me.

I feel so much pain, so much sorrow,

Will it ever be better, maybe tomorrow,

I have wished to die before but not today.

I have to stay here I simply need to stay.

I have a pain deep within my heart.

It started to heal, but my worlds are torn apart.

I wish I knew what it was I needed,

But I constantly feel like I am mistreated.

I feel so tired of the endless game of lies,

That I do sometimes wonder what it be like to die.

These thoughts I know you should not mention,

Although everyone I know Is afraid that they have them.

I am strong I will survive through this,

But sometimes I wonder if that makes any sense,

I need someone to me loved unconditionally and freely,

Simply for who I am not because someone wants to change me,

I found that love and it made me so happy,

But I'm not sure I'd have recognized it before if you asked me.

SHADOWS OF LOVE

In the ancient shadows of love, I wait for heartache,

It seems no one can understand; How I love or feel today.

. . .

I am a mystery that is kept secure and far away,

As the breeze runs by, I am left to feel upset on this day.

In my darkest sadness, I see heartbreak,

I wonder if it is possible for me to escape.

If silent shadows slip by, to me they say nay.

Yet, I think they wish me love, if only for one more day.

I would rather leave this world, and take my love far away,

So that we would know happiness and forget about heartache.

It seems to me that people never know what to say,

But it is rather obvious they don't wish love for me today.

THE END

In the deepest darkness of the mind,

After she has ensured she is all alone she cries,

And she wonders if this is all life is to be,

And if it is she wishes her life forfeit to the sea,

And all her dreams, all but a few came true,

Yet tonight she dances, and you never knew.

That tonight she would take her life in her hands,

Tonight, she decided she had enough of this dance.

Some would say it is weakness that makes one act this way,

But she grew tired of all the games they played.

And one night even though she knew she was loved,

She took her life, hoping there was a happy ever after above.

She would leave a note "don't blame yourself",

For I, my friends, was beyond your help.

I was different and free and lost in the sea,

And sometimes felt as if no one ever really knew me.

LONELY

Lonely is a feeling that I know well,

It screams inside my head so very loud.

Lonely is a feeling that hurts me so much,

I feel alienated, depressed and so far, apart.

Loneliness is a feeling that won't go away.

It comes to haunt you almost every day.

Loneliness is a feeling that harbors so much pain.

I tried as hard as I could but couldn't escape.

Loneliness is a feeling you feel all of the time.

Others try to be there, but this loneliness is mine.

Lonely is that feeling, more than just being alone.

No one seemed to listen and no one seems at home.

Lonely is a that something that creeps into your heart,

And slowly everyday tears your heart and mind apart.

Lonely is that feeling that grabs you and won't let go.

Loneliness inside you can drag you down so very low,

Loneliness is that feeling have because of love.

A love that hurts you is sometimes just too much.

THE STRUGGLE

The ache it lances through my heart and soul,

Scouring my body and mind for that which it stole.

It leaves me feeling bent and broken in hopes I'll let go,

Knowing once I do, it will own me, and I will be alone.

I stand even though I am bent with pain and agony,

I cry but I hold as tightly as ever to my sanity,

I feel myself slipping and my balance is wavering,

I am reaching for someone or something to save me.

Even deep in this despair I still find some light of hope,

It rages and wars with the feeling that it cannot be so.

I know that this darkness will either consume me or pass,

It is in my hands, and it is my fate, I have only to ask.

He reaches from his world to mine to lend me his hand,

I have doubts about if I should take it, yet I can barely stand.

He could be dangerous, this could end badly, yet here I am.

There must come a point when I must learn to trust again.

. . .

The wind is howling from the pain that twists through my soul,

The war rages on within, to regain what the monsters stole.

I will prevail, I will be strong, I will heal, I will it to be so.

I took his hand and I am safe now, I am alone and not alone.

BECAUSE IT WAS UNCOMFORTABLE

Because it was uncomfortable,

They never told me the risks.

They never said suicide,

was the second highest cause of death.

Even if I had been told,

I can't say it would have made a difference.

Because it's uncomfortable,

We're trained to pretend it doesn't exist.

Because it was uncomfortable,

they hid the fact that he liked little boys and girls,

there is plenty of outrage at others,

but you hide it when it's one of yours.

Because it was uncomfortable,

they blamed the victim instead,

Maybe it was the clothes she wore,

or perhaps it's all in her head.

Because it was uncomfortable,

they fumbled around those in grief,

Making people feel inadequate.

when they ought to encourage them to grieve.

Because it was uncomfortable,

that tragedy struck suddenly.

They threw together solutions,

that wouldn't actually benefit anybody.

Because it was uncomfortable,

they turned a blind eye to many things,

Leading to the downfall,

of goodness and letting the evil seep in.

Because it was uncomfortable,

looking at the past through the years,

They sought to destroy all reminders,

as if it could erase already cried tears.

Because it was uncomfortable,

for even one person in any way,

Everyone was asked,

to adapt until communication itself went away.

Because it was uncomfortable,

we enabled and became more extreme,

The utopia we tried to build,

became a memory and we were far from free.

THE DARKNESS AND THE MAIDEN

It is truly a shame that we don't give emotions their due.

Many spend a large part of their life just trying to get through.

When you are young you don't always see the connections,

To your behaviors and those traumatic past inflictions.

Wondering why the darkness seemed so oppressive,

Not even remembering all the bad, the mind being repressive,

A tactic it uses to try and be reactively protective,

But it leads to many having a misunderstood or wrong diagnosis.

So, the maiden can't recall all of what has harmed her,

But she eventually comes to understand that she needs some armor,

Unfortunately, she is still too quick to trust and take it off,

And she swings wildly from being too tough to too soft.

She found herself feeling more of a misfit, someone misunderstood,

Which made her more susceptible to someone slick and assured.

Older men still found her, and because she didn't quite fit in with her age,

It was easy for them, telling her things, making her feel less strange.

It all made sense, if she didn't belong with all of the other kids,

All he had to do was swoop in and tell her how mature she is,

And it resonates because she felt like an outsider so rings like truth,

When really it was just manipulation setting her up for abuse.

She was always seeking temporary relief from the aching hole in her heart.

With no parents to guide her, she had tried to make her own start.

But she would chameleon to what she thought they wanted her to be.

Trying to show them only what she knew they wanted to see.

She craved an attention that brought about the wrong kinds of looks,

The kind that later, they would use to let a predator off the hook.

Society likes to blame the victim when things get too uncomfortable,

She would never admit, indeed I don't think she knew, she was vulnerable.

Relief and changes only came when she started therapy,

And she started working on her trauma with regularity,

She noticed the darkness shifted and got lighter the more she worked.

She became more comfortable with herself as she started healing the hurt.

THE DARKNESS AND THE MOTHER

There is no Mother that would truly wish to see her child consumed,

By the darkest of feelings leaving them bereft and confused.

All she ever seeks is to protect them from anything that'd mean them harm,

And sometimes no matter how hard she tries she misses the mark.

Concerned with her children she might miss the grip the darkness has on her,

Until it's too late and she's uncertain to whom she might be able to turn.

Her role has been as a caregiver for her entire life, she knows nothing else,

So, she might be tempted to ignore the signs and further neglect herself.

The danger in ignoring the feelings is that they rarely go away on their own.

Ignoring them tends to compound them making them more powerful.

Stay busy and focus on the kids, as long as they are okay, I'll be okay too,

You wonder when they struggle, will your love be enough to help see them through?

Then one day if they are gone from your life, will you be able to survive?

Empty nests, and losses, would indicate it's more likely you'd feel deprived.

Lost and floating in a vast empty space, a void left where they once were,

Will you choose to help yourself, will you choose to heal from this hurt.

THE DARKNESS AND THE CRONE

All the years of feelings and experiences,

Have taught you much about the art of avoidance.

You no longer feel the need to busy away the darkness,

You've accept it's role in our lives, perhaps made friends.

Grief will come for every single one of us in one way or another,

You know avoiding it forever is simply impossible,

It's better to understand that there are healthy ways to grieve,

Knowing that it's normal, learning to make space for it, can bring peace.

The other dark feelings like shame and blame you let go,

They still fight for space sometimes but they are a familiar foe,

You know their weakness is self compassion and love,

As you live in the moment, giving the past a good shove.

Occasionally that sadness and depressions sneak in,

Wanting to steal your joy and trying to tuck you in a tailspin.

But you know that your emotions are not your enemy,

And acknowledging that sadness can lead to serenity.

By giving space to your emotions and working with them,

You find yourself often able to determine from where they stem.

The root of the emotions is often the most powerful point,

And so much healing can take place just giving them a voice.

Your Darkness Fighting Free-Writing:

I invite you to join me in a free writing session.

Have you ever had a struggle with any negative emotions? I invite you to write about anything that moves you. What speaks to your soul?

Your Darkness Poem

YOUR DARKNESS POEM

I invite you to read through your free writing and look for any poetry in it. Use it as inspiration to write your own *Darkness Fighting* poems or just let the poetry flow through you. Sometimes circling words that rhyme can help you see patterns.

Self-Esteem

Though My Self-Esteem,
Entirely battered and bruised,
I began healing

L ooking back through my poetry was like watching a movie replay. Only this time, I had the benefit of all the wisdom. I can see where I gave too much of myself; I can see where I was co-dependent or unhealthy. Trying so hard to fill a void that no one else could fill but me. This chapter is filled with poetry written from insecurities, low self-esteem, and doubt. I lacked the self-compassion and self-love I desperately needed. Worse, at the time, I thought I did love myself, but I didn't really know what self-love was. I couldn't see it quite yet. As I grew and healed, I began to see and accept my flaws and faults. I began to understand that I held myself, at times, to impossible standards. I understood that I desperately wanted love, but it took time to realize, the love I needed was from myself. I hope, if you have ever struggled with your own self-worth the words here will help you feel less alone, encourage self-compassion, and encourage you on your journey.

INSECURITY

Who is that,

That girl that called?

Was she calling,

Because you wanted her to call?

Who is that,

That girl that you mentioned?

Did you mention her,

Because you always wanted her?

Who is that,

That girl from your past?

Two years have gone by,

They can seem to go fast.

Who is that,

that called today?

Is it the girl,

You knew from another day?

Who is that,

That person who said hi,

Another two years,

Have slowly went by.

Who is that,

That girl that you liked?

Why does she call,

Here so late at night?

Who is that,

The girl from before?

Do you still want her,

How much do you want her?

Who is that,

That girl that I saw,

Is she your type?

Will you leave me by fall?

Who is that,

That girl you were with?

You were with her before,

What makes this time so different?

Who is that,

That girl that called?

Tell me right now,

Will you leave me at all?

Who is that,

That girl who just left?

What was she doing,

With her arms around your neck.

Who is that,

That girl that you want?

What happened to me,

Do I mean nothing at all?

I'M ME

Who are you to judge me,

And who are you to say,

That I can't be this way?

And what right do you have,

With your narrow minds,

To look at me and laugh?

Well I want you to know,

That I won't ever go!

I'm still the same....So,

I think that you should leave,

With your petty thoughts,

Just leave me here to be.

'Cause I can be myself,

And you will never see,

Just how good that it can be, simply to be free.

Cause your still caught inside,

Locked inside yourself,

Afraid to simply be, afraid to be like me.

Afraid to know the truth,

Afraid to be yourself,

And now you're someone else.

NOT REALLY SURE

I'm not really sure,

Just where to go from here,

And I'm not really sure,

Just how much you really care.

All I know right now,

Is that you have gone away?

All I'm really sure of,

Is it that you couldn't stay.

Now you've left me all alone,

and I am left here with no one.

So where do I go when I feel blue,

There's no one for me to run to.

I'm not really sure,

Just where to go from here,

And I'm not really sure,

If anybody really cares.

All I know right now,

Is that I need someone to hold me,

All I am really sure of,

Is it that I feel so very lonely?

EVERYONE LOVES HER

There is a girl for every guy,

At least, that's what they say.

There's a girl a guy wants,

In their own separate way.

They say they love you,

And they really mean to be true,

But there's always at least one girl,

He loves in a different way from you.

Everyone loves her,

She's everything you're not.

Everyone loves her,

She's always in his thoughts.

He might be with you,

But his thoughts are with her,

You must prepare yourself,

And be ready for the hurt.

He won't stay much longer,

He has seen her too often,

And now he can't help himself,

Or his feelings of wanting.

Soon, he'll leave you far behind,

With only thoughts of her in his mind,

He will hurt you; it's in his nature,

Just to be excited by a stranger.

I FEEL

I feel alone,

And there is nothing I can do.

I feel alone,

And I really need you.

I feel so sad,

And I can't tell you why.

I feel so sad,

And it's killing me inside.

If I feel happy,

It's all because of you.

If I feel happy,

I know you love me too.

When I feel sad,

I just can't let you know,

When I feel sad,

My sadness just seems to grow.

When I feel alone,

I really want you to hold me.

When I feel lonely,

I just want you to be with me.

I WANT TO BE THE ONE

I want to be THE ONE,

The one he will do anything for,

The one he can't forget,

The one he thinks about all the time,

The one he misses when he's not around,

The one he wants to comfort and protect,

The one he wants to shelter from the evil of the world.

The one he wants to hold and caress,

The one he wants to see smile,

The one he can't stand when she's mad,

The one that never wants to see her sad,

The one that he can't see his life without.

CONFLICTED

Like the brilliant and powerful sunlight,

Like the healing moon that shines at night.

It's here, it's gone, love's disappeared,

Leaving me grieving just as you feared.

In this world, there is no mercy,

You should have had better boundaries,

No more love, it's lost its light,

This world is becoming as dark as night,

If you are different, then you're called a freak,

If you're the same, you're considered weak.

You don't seem to be able to win this game,

So just be yourself, it's better that way.

Happiness never lasts for long these days,

It hits me, like my grief, in waves.

Violence has taken over, and evil is rising,

Will the good prevail? Will we keep fighting?

Fate, faith, lies, and betrayal are all connected.

Good and evil cannot live without each other unaffected.

Sadness has taken over your soul, but you wish to be happy.

Perhaps having faith in yourself and loving yourself is the key.

ONCE MORE

I slid,

Falling freely,

Into the darkness,

That'd continue to consume me.

I cried,

Tears flowing,

Into the heartache,

That he would inflict unknowing.

I raged,

Against all,

From my past,

That had come to call.

I bent,

Doubled over,

In immeasurable pain,

Realizing I couldn't be her.

I broke,

Like before,

Entirely left alone,

I wasn't enough once more.

LONELY CREATURE

She is a creature who is alone,

Nowhere has she found another like she,

She is a being who feels solitude whole,

Never has she seen another she.

She walked through the earth in isolation, alone,

She sees beauty in nature, and there she finds love,

Still, she walks through life alone,

Feeling as though she will never have intimate love.

She is a creature who is unique,

Anyone else like her, there could not be,

She is a being entirely made different,

And for that, she suffers a lonely existence.

She has traveled through time and space, it seems,

To become this creature that you see,

She has traveled through love, hate, and tragedy,

To learn to love herself completely unseen.

Still, sadness overtakes her as she sits to think,

She will never have the love of another,

Anger becomes a byproduct inside as she thinks,

She is eternally alone, so why bother?

ALL ALONE

A girl sits all alone,

She wishes on a star,

That very little star,

That goes so very far.

Love is lost,

And never found,

This girl I know,

Who lives around?

She's here and there,

And everywhere,

At every time,

She's in the air.

They left her time,

And time again,

They left her,

With very few friends.

They left her,

One by one,

She knew they'd go,

It wasn't fun.

All alone, all alone,

The words go through her head,

All alone, all alone,

She lies alone in bed.

All alone, all alone,

This lonely girl feels dead,

Look around, and you will see,

There's a girl like this in everybody.

All alone, all alone,

Why do people leave people all alone?

Nobody but nobody,

Can make it all alone.

LONELY

Lonely is a feeling that I know well.

It screams inside my head so very loud.

Lonely is a feeling that hurts me so much,

I feel alienated, depressed, and so far apart.

Lonely is a feeling that won't go away.

It comes to haunt you almost every day.

Lonely is a feeling that harbors so much pain.

I tried as hard as I could but couldn't escape.

Lonely is a feeling you feel all of the time.

Others try to be there, but this loneliness is mine.

Lonely is that feeling, more than just being alone.

No one seems to listen, and no one seems at home.

Lonely is something that creeps into your heart.

And slowly every day tears your heart and mind apart.

Lonely is that feeling that grabs you and won't let go.

Loneliness inside you can drag you down so very low,

Lonely is that feeling I have because of love.

A love that hurts you is sometimes just too much.

UNIQUE CREATURE

I am a creature who is alone,

Nowhere have I found another like I.

I am a being who is alone,

Never have I seen anyone feel like I.

I walk through this earth alone,

I see beauty in nature, and I find love.

I walk through life alone,

I will never have an intimate love.

I am a creature who is unique,

I cannot be anyone else but me.

I am a being who is different,

And for that, no one seems to let me be.

I traveled through time and space, it seems,

To become this creature that you see.

I traveled through love, hate, and tragedy,

To come to myself and to love.

Sadness overtakes me now as I think,

I will never have the love of another.

Anger is a byproduct inside, as I think,

I am alone, so why should I bother?

I've asked myself why.

Why am I so different?

No one seems to love me,

And I feel like a star, distant.

I've wondered to myself,

Why does time stand still,

In some of the worst moments,

But flies by the others seemingly at will?

PEOPLE PLEASER

Surrounded by loneliness and abandonment,

I tried to get rid of feeling this.

I need to feel special, one of a kind.

I need to feel as if I'm worth the time.

Never was I like everyone else,

Never was there someone who understood.

That the way my mind works is not like yours,

I'm trapped in myself with no remorse.

I need to feel loved and whole and complete,

I need to feel as if others have a need for me.

The way it seems the world would be better without me,

But I am too stubborn to just let it be.

I am in love, and that keeps me sane.

For a time, I thought nothing would stop this pain.

Sometimes, love will cause you pain as well,

But in pain without love is not for me to dwell.

PUZZLING

Isn't it funny how people,

Need to feel needed and important to someone?

How unreasonable a thought can be,

How unreasonable expectations can be.

It is better to expect nothing or less

So as to not be hurt or disappointed.

How important am I, exactly?

How many people need me to be here?

Too many people need me,

But are not there when I need them.

Just because I do something

That doesn't mean the favor is returned.

Just because I need it

Doesn't mean someone else does and will give it.

My constant need for attention is tearing me up inside,

Sometimes, I wonder if it will ever be satisfied.

My need to feel loved and important ties in with attention,

Abandonment issues won't let go of any of them.

Sometimes loneliness can be your friend.

SECOND GUESSES

Second, Solitude, secrets, serene, sad,

Lies, love, lonely, lost, left, last.

Alone, afraid, Abandoned

Why, in my silence, do I scream?

When I know that no one hears me?

When they hear me, they still don't listen?

And I become even more alone and abandoned.

I found my fairy tale, or I had thought.

Until I realized that fairytales are false.

Do I really want to be happy at all?

Why can't I think things are wonderful?

Always, I place second, never first,

Should it matter? Why should I feel hurt?

CHAOS

*** Awarded the Editor's Choice Award by the International Library of Poetry

Spiraling out of control,

Lost in a world of thoughtlessness,

Forgotten my all above and below,

Stranded inside myself, listless.

I scream silent screams,

No one hears me cry for help,

Stuck in my whirlwind of loneliness,

All I can do is find myself.

Lost in the middle of chaos,

I am gripped by frustration,

Held close by death himself,

I am swept further into isolation.

I spiral into the heart of my tornado,

Grasping at anything, I have only my will,

I am looking for the eye of the storm,

Waiting for the chaos to leave me still.

BE THERE FOR MYSELF

Always, it seems I break down, and no one is there.

It seems sometimes like no one really cares.

I tried to be positive and stay in good spirits.

But people like to shut me down for their kicks.

I lost so much, and still, I lose more.

Again, I find I want to close the door.

I am alone when it comes right down to it,

And in this loneliness, my heart doesn't fit.

I cried myself to sleep every night this week,

To find that even now, my eyes still leak.

Tell me what I did so wrong and if I am that bad,

That I deserve to feel like this, to feel so sad?

I have all I can do to fight against this despair,

But still, even as I write this, I feel it in the air.

My heart is filled with anguish that cannot be rivaled,

As I fight to stay calm, the pain is so frightful.

I need someone to hold me and tell me it is okay,

But there is no one here for me, no, not today.

PATH TO PASSIONS

Season changing, the seasons done,

Now I'm here remembering what it was,

Got to keep on moving everything will change.

Hated by what it once was, I fade away.

So strong and so weak no one sees,

I'm trapped here where no one sees me.

Stumbling blind, searching for things that hide,

My way to my passions I am determined to find.

SIMPLE FLOWER

I'm a simple flower,

Floating on the breeze.

You can try to catch me,

You can try to see,

But you will never understand.

Just where my beauty lies,

To see you must look with more than eyes.

THIS GIRL I KNOW

She wears a long flowing dress,

Hair flowing with the wind from her head.

Her blue eyes sparkle like a fresh spring,

And feels as though this is a new beginning.

Her smile warms the hearts of those around,

Those who love her never want to see her frown

Her love of laughter is clear in her eyes

The same eyes that match the color of the sky

This girl is light-hearted and free

She dances and twirls like the falling leaves

She smiles as the wind caresses her face

And she feels as though she's from a different place

For the moment, she dances around the trees

She feels not hurt or pain, only harmony

She knows that in nature, she is truly free

This girl I know, I feel it could be me.

ALONE

Left alone in the darkness, I have become a part of the void.

The rift that grows larger leaves my heart feeling cold.

Alone in this world of chaos and deception,

I am out of place, lost, and frequently abandoned.

In the candle-lit night, as the moon shines on me,

I dance and sing and finally feel some inner peace.

Harsh lessons of life teach me I am truly alone,

There is no fairy tale romance; there is no home.

VICIOUS CIRCLE

It's a vicious circle that I find myself in,

Feeling insecure is so unattractive.

I feel insecure because I might be unattractive,

Yet, I am unattractive because I am insecure.

There is no way to gracefully stop this cycle,

I can only continue to try.

I'M NOT BROKEN, I'M BROKEN

The girl sang a song called broken,

But in another said not to fix here,

She was not broken but she was,

Refusing to give in to despairs very touch.

I hear her voice, I feel exactly as she does,

Defiantly struggling against the possibility, rebellious,

Fighting against my self as I take his words to heart,

Feeling them pull me into the darkness and tear me apart.

If I were normal would I be bulletproof,

Would I be able to absorb it all or let it bounce off,

Instead it roots itself, and drags me down,
Confirming I'm not good enough it wants me to drown.

Suffocating, I fight, looking for air, for a little light,

How have I become surrounded by the darkness gain,

How could I allow him the control by touch of hand,

When will I stop cowering from the onslaught and take a stand.

She said "Love, I don't know love." and I felt the truth,

I didn't know love, I only knew being used.

My worth inextricably tied to my body and my light,

I was someone to use for sex or I was there for them to destroy.

They wanted my innocence and my light,

Because it made them happy to see it destroyed,

They would suck all of the light from souls,

But I wouldn't let them, they didn't get to have that hold.

But now, now my light is dim and darkness, surrounded me,

As all the evils caught up to me when I stopped running,

I stopped to face them all, foolish girl that I am,

Because I know I can't defeat them if I also have to fight him.

My intentions were to heal, for me, for him,

But I made it worse and he can't understand,

It's one step forward and a stair case back,

My struggle to heal makes me feel broken and more worthless at last.

So I sit writing frivolous words, likely never to be seen,

Still trying to stop the darkness from crushing me,

Trying to remember we are all worth so much more,

Than what one person might believe after all that's only one door.

I WANNA BE THE GIRL

I hear a song about a girl a guy loves,

He sings about her and her soft touch,

In every song, he is enamored and captivated,

The thought of losing her brings devastation.

He sings about the ways that she moves,

And she always brings out his best moods,

He always feels passion, and he wants her forever,

He loves every little thing about her.

I always wanted a love just like that,

One that would always have my back,

A guy that loved me enough to never leave,

And also, could feel for me just as deeply,

I've been told that love doesn't exist,

Songs are just songs, and that is it,

I'll never be the girl that the guy sings about,

I'm made of crazy, passion, and self-doubt.

But I want to be that girl for him,

The one that captivates and haunts him,

I want to be the girl he can never leave,

Because his life will always be better with me.

I want to be the girl he always wants,

The one he feels he has to take into his arms,

I want to be the girl he can't live without,

The one whose flame of passion will never go out.

HOW MANY TIMES

How many times did love turn to betrayal?

How many times did you fall?

Hoping someone would protect your heart,

How many times did you give them all?

And the scars you hide ache even more,

As you stand in front of the door.

Wondering what's right or wrong,

And what's worth living for?

STOP AND STAND STILL

Stop and stand still,

You're moving too far away from your peace.

You are running and running, and your tank is on empty.

Stop and Stand Still,

Reach for the stars,

You keep running and forgetting who you really are.

Stop and stand still,

Don't let others stop you from being unique,

To be different and free is your blessing.

ALWAYS SECOND

Utterly alone and afraid,

Left behind, lost, and ashamed,

Saddened and hurt by love, I cry,

And no one hears or sees the lie.

It's true that animals' sense hurt,

Mine come to me for comfort,

I have lost everything that I had,

Life spirals out of control, so sad.

Unrealistic expectations hold true,

Until the end when they die hard, too.

You stop to wonder if you are important,

No, not to them, not this morning.

Lies, deceit, and misery surround me,

I can't live this life around me,

I fall into a tornado of emotion,

Struggling to be the understanding one.

I've tried, I gave, I cried, I fell,

There is nothing left of this dry well,

I've had enough of this turbulence,

No one would notice my disappearance.

Priorities do not include me at all,

I fall to the side, and further I fall.

So hurt by the casualties extended,

I do not wish to be taken for granted.

Still, I sit and write away,

Hoping to escape all my pain,

Second, I come to everyone else,

In the eyes of the one to whom I fell.

PULLED

Pulled in every direction away from myself, away from my center,

There begins the general spiral downward, falling forever.

Eager to please everyone else, to put them all first and foremost,

Pieces of me are torn and ripped, scattered with the windy gusts.

If I fall, it will be my own doing, and I know no one will see it happen,

I won't reach out for help, I won't be a burden, I won't hear them laughing.

NOT TOUGH ENOUGH

She felt like an orphan; in a sense, she was,

The one person who watched over her was lost,

Now alone in the world, she had to be tough,

Sometimes she wished being tough was enough.

Every year, there were different faces, different friends,

Hardly anyone lasting longer than five years at best,

Loquacious and garrulous, she would rant and rave,

Trying to fill the silence, to quiet the depression and rage.

Successful at first but unsuccessful in the end,

She thought perhaps that the darkness would win,

This was an eternal struggle she found herself in,

She could not bring in others to help her win.

Who would she turn to in her hours of need,

When no one understood her, or so it had seemed,

So quick to be angry with her or ignore her completely,

So quick to give up and walk away or judge her as needy.

She was a girl with a heart that always let you in,

She was easily hurt, but she would also easily forgive,

She was growing and learning, but it wasn't enough,

After it all, she decided she just wasn't that tough.

COME CLOSER

Come closer,

To the darkest levels that no one else has touched,

To the furthest place from the light that no one else has loved.

I JUST NEEDED A DAD

You were supposed to protect me,

Not be the one who caused me harm,

You were supposed to be there,

I should have felt safe in your arms.

You were supposed to protect me,

I wasn't supposed to grow up so fast,

It was your job to keep me safe,

I shouldn't have gone through all that I have.

You were supposed to teach me,

Not give me bad examples and absences,

You were supposed to show me,

That I was worth more, especially to them.

You were supposed to teach me,

How a man should treat a lady,

You were supposed to lead by example

So that I would learn it daily.

She was supposed to teach me,

Everything I needed about being a woman,

But you were supposed to teach me,

That I could be valued and loved by somebody.

I put so much of the blame on her; I didn't see,

I couldn't begin to understand it until now,

How critical your role was to a little girl, to me,

You were gone, and I still don't understand how.

You were supposed to keep me safe,

But you didn't, instead, you focused on yourself,

Now I don't know how to fix all you have broken,

You were supposed to be the one who would always help.

Did she make you feel less important,

Or did you just one day decide to give me up?

How could you not see how important your role was?

You'll never understand the damage that you've done.

You were supposed to teach me my worth,

My value and all I have to offer,

But I just feel like I'm never enough.

Who would want to stay with me, not even my fathers?

To have my own Dad become estranged,

That didn't happen just once, no, not for me,

You could blame my mom, but it doesn't change,

I had two dads who would ultimately pack up and leave.

And now I'll hold you accountable for yourself,

See, I've been trying to fix the mess you made in my head.

I might have even found someone that will help,

I just wish I wasn't so afraid that I'm not enough after all is said.

See what you really showed me by leaving like you did,

Is that men don't stay, there is no loyalty,

And I would be better served to keep my heart hid,

Lest I fall in love to be left in the midst of anxiety,

You didn't show me what I was really worth,

I went out and tried to find that for myself,

I am stronger than your absence, than your loss,

And I still love with every piece of my heart.

And with all that love I give to someone I think is worthy,

Comes all the turmoil and anxiety that it still isn't enough,

And I'm more likely to be hurt or be left feeling lonely,

All because I refuse not to love the way I love.

So, I survive in spite of your absence,

In spite of your lack of attention or protection,

But how you treated me caused so much damage,

That I can't fix it with just this poem of introspection.

Instead, I sit here, and recognize that I didn't acknowledge your role,

In fact, I rejected it, and any meaning it might have had in my life.

Until I was faced with mortality until I thought about marriage,

When I realized all these years why I accepted men who were less than nice.

How could I know it wasn't okay to be treated so bad,

You were not there to show me the difference,

I had no frame of reference, that there was more to be had,

You failed me in this, and in so much more, as I realized I needed a dad.

PROGRESSION OF LOVE

I would have loved him, if I had known how,

But I was confused and my world upside down.

Traumatic changes and death were all around,

I was vulnerable and lost, and I felt I might drown.

I would have loved him, with all my heart and soul,

And what great adventures we could have had,

But he lied, and he cheated, and I let this one go,

With no desire to mend the trust that was broken so.

I would have realized what I felt was not love,

When he grabbed my throat, squeezing the air from my lungs,

Sometimes screaming if I can't have you, no one can,

But I was insecure and lost, and that was all I knew and had.

I would still love him if he had shown me affection,

But he needed so much more space than I could give,

Content with online worlds and time with friends,

And I was still broken from the last, and I could not give.

I would still love him if only he were here,

But he was taken from this world, gone now for years,

He was kind and understanding and knew me well,

If we had more time, we didn't, and I have none on which to dwell.

I would still love him if he had let me,

I could have given him every piece of me,

But he pushed and pulled, always undecided,

With each push, the wounds deepen, and love starts dying.

I would have still loved him if he were nice,

But every word was venomous and filled with spite,

He could not seem to find a way to speak right,

And I would not keep someone who could not be nice.

I would have loved him if only it were allowed,

But it simply could not be, not then and not now.

He seemed the perfect match, but I could not rewrite his past.

He has found someone far better than me, a perfect match.

I would have loved them all before I loved myself,

I didn't have examples of love; I was always seeking it out,

That is why fathers have an important role to play,

Do your job right, and your daughters won't make these mistakes.

PRECIOUS GIRL

I wish I could show you how to be treated right,

Never let man nor friend dim your beautiful light.

You are so very precious just the way you are,

If they don't see it, let them go. I know it is hard.

But you do not deserve to feel in any way less than,

If someone makes you feel that way often, that is not a friend.

When you are looking for true love, you will be hurt,

I cannot save you from this even if these words were heard.

I'll say them anyway: if he doesn't make you smile, he's not the one,

You should never settle or accept abuse from anyone.

It can be hard to see when you are in the middle, be careful,

You should feel happy and loved more often than you feel awful.

Finally, never accept someone who tells you that you are not enough,

It might be true for them, but trust me, someone else is dying for your love.

SELF-REFLECTION

It is so interesting to have the words before me,

To see the pain I was feeling so clearly.

Watching as I worked out some of the sources,

No longer mysterious and hidden forces.

There is a certain revelation that comes with time,

If you've done the work, not just stumbling by,

When you look back, you can see the patterns and the roots,

You can step outside of yourself, no longer making it about you.

Taking the ego away, looking at simply what was,

I think this is something that could benefit all of us.

Watching the victim mentality and being proud of my growth,

Seeing it creep in even as that growth unfolds.

Accepting all of who you are, renaming your flaws,

If they are a part of you, are they flaws at all?

I suppose that would come down to if you are happy,

A bit of a challenge to say yes if you struggle with self-esteem.

But what if our self-esteem issues all came from wanting validation,

And what if we didn't need that anymore? What a transformation.

And what if we gave ourselves all that love we felt we were missing,

Then maybe we could stop picking the wrong person for kissing.

I had to acknowledge that my childhood was colorful,

But I had to be careful and use it to move forward, not as an excuse.

It's completely terrible that anyone should ever know abuse,

But by acknowledging it and healing, I could stop the cycle of misuse.

Finally, I realized, that my inner child never felt safe,

So, I had to work out better self-care until that becomes the case,

And I had to work with the parts of me that were misused,

Trying to correct all of the beliefs about myself that were misconstrued.

All the stories and agreements I had made before my brain was developed,

That no longer served me and needed my attention to be redeveloped,

And for every part of me that was shattered, I had to carefully pour gold,

To fill in all the cracks to heal and piece back my soul.

A POETIC LETTER TO MY CHILDHOOD SELF

You deserved to be a child, to laugh and to play,

You deserved to always, and I mean always be safe.

It's not your fault that men, with their twisted and perverted ways,

Crossed boundaries and worse while telling you it was just play.

You didn't ask for any of the things that happened to you,

Nor were you responsible for their actions towards you,

It was not because "you're so pretty" or "such a good girl",

It was because of broken men in a broken world.

You've been caring for more than your share since you were ten years old.

When you should have been playing and listening to stories told.

I know you were excited to have a little sister when they first told you,

But as the years went by there were just more and more tasks to do.

You became a caretaker, and housecleaner, expected to get perfect grades,

Playtime became less and less, as grown-up tasks filled your days,

It wasn't your fault they asked so much of you so young,

You deserved to be out with others your age laughing and having fun.

It wasn't your fault when you found yourself alone with that older guy,

Going from such a strict household to one that left you to your devices,

You deserved to be protected from this kind of danger,

Regardless of how you dress or even flirty behavior.

Had they taken the time to understand the trauma of your past,

Or simply how different your brain was wired from the rest,

They may have seen that you saw your behavior as being nice,

Not an invitation to indulge in someone else's vice.

It wasn't your fault they saw you as an adult when you were a child,

Or that they couldn't face the skeletons in the closet and stayed in denial,

You didn't wish for any of this, encourage it, or make it happen,

What you needed and deserved was protection and compassion.

Life certainly wasn't fair when your second dad abandoned you,

Then your mom sent you away from the only home you knew,

After that, you were angry and refused to come back home,

Convinced that if you had to you would live your life all alone.

It's not your fault that your mom passed from this world to the next,

I know you think you could have healed her, could have helped her rest,

If only you'd gone back home, you could take care of her again,

And she'd still be here, and perhaps it would ease all your discontent.

I know you were desperate for love and very naive,

You didn't deserve to be treated badly or beat.

It wasn't your fault, you're brain wasn't developed completely,

You chose the wrong people and gave your love too freely.

You were still a child, but believed yourself to be grown,

Holding yourself to standards you couldn't possibly have known,

Causing yourself more damage as you piled on the shame,

Willingly absorbing and accepting all of the blame.

The truth is you deserved to be protected and cared for,

And you deserved to be loved even more.

A POETIC LETTER TO MYSELF

I know you think you'll be all grown up the second you hit eighteen,

But by the time you're thirty, you'll realize you were still in between,

Still growing and learning, and changing your mind with ease,

So certain you had all the answers, offering your expertise.

I'm sorry that you didn't have a dad to show you how you should be loved,

It wasn't your fault you kept picking the wrong guys unable to accurately judge,

Convinced you could fill the void in your heart by giving them more love,

Unable to see that the more you gave, the more damage they wrought.

It wasn't your fault when someone you trusted kept pouring drinks,

And someone slipped something in one making it hard to think,

I know the violation that you felt led to an oppressive darkness,

That could have cost you your life but it saved it instead.

I think it is amazing that you keep getting up every day and dreaming,

Refusing to give up, working hard, and searching for life's meaning.

You can't save everyone, you can't help everyone, I know you can't help but try,

Most of the time it led to pain, heartache, and sacrifice,

I know you question if the decisions you made were right,

But those decisions are already made so it couldn't be anything else.

Pain comes from too much focus on the past or the future,

If you could have done more you would have, nothing is truer,

You've had plenty of compassion for everyone else,

Now it's time to cultivate self-compassion for yourself.

THE INSECURE MAIDEN

This tumultuous life is to blame for my feeling insecure,

I was taught that I had to be perfect to make it in this world.

Always falling short; everyone pointing out all my flaws,

Making me feel even less adequate; why should I try all?

But I cannot stop myself from giving everything I've got,

I feel everything to such a severe magnification,

Set even further apart as everyone around me feels dissimilar,

I can seem to relate; life should be so much simpler.

In many of my relationships, I would end up feeling like a prisoner,

While they took everything I had, demanding more, being particular.

I didn't have an example of what a healthy relationship looked like,

It would be trial and error while I discovered the hard way what I disliked.

Choosing more people to fill my life with, similar to those I knew,

Turned into a massive mistake and set me up for stackable sets of abuse.

Sending me to do even more healing when each relationship ended.

Worse, that I could only be with someone I felt an emotional attachment?

I've never quite been like the rest of my friends, who could date casually,

I have no idea if this was part of or contributed to my state of self-esteem.

But the abuse I endured as a child made me switch to the extremes,

As a teen, I would have been promiscuous, but I came close to celibacy.

I seemed to be holding myself responsible for decisions I made as a child,

Thinking myself grown, and blaming myself for when I'd be defiled.

I remember thinking back then; I was so mature for my age,

But I was really just an easy mark for a predator to engage.

By the time I really started to understand, It was still a long road ahead,

There was so much work to do for the healing to be had,

But I can tell you know just as surely as I breathe,

It was worth all the hard work to finally feel more complete.

And sure, my brain still doesn't work like many others,

Now that I have healed, I see it has some superpowers,

Because of all I've been through, I have a lot more empathy,

And now that I've accepted the lessons, I have a better eye for safety.

THE UNCERTAIN MOTHER

If I could go back and tell my kids valuable lessons,

I would tell them to find people and friends who really listen.

Hopefully, they would have learned good qualities from being with me,

But being a single parent, that masculine role was still lacking,

I did my best, I had an amazing friend that became family,

And he stepped in to fill that role of masculinity,

But children are funny sometimes they don't see,

blinded by their expectations of what they thought should be.

If I could go back and give myself some advice,

I'd start with, unless you love yourself no other love will suffice.

That black hole you feel that you want someone else to fill,

You have to give yourself all that love, it won't be filled until.

I'd give all the love I could to the child within my own heart,

At the earliest age I could, it is never too early to start.

Embark on a journey of healing as soon as you feel ready,

Never be ashamed or hesitant to seek out professional therapy.

When someone says something that makes you react emotionally,

Get curious and ask yourself "Why does this affect me?"

Is there something in what they said in which you are in agreement,

And is that agreement true, and do you really need it?

Never let anyone tell you that you are unworthy of love,

Love is meant for each and every one of us.

If someone tried to make you feel in any way less than you are,

That is a sign that it is time for your ways to part.

No one has the right to physically abuse you, ever.

Defend yourself, cut all ties, and never accept this behavior.

If you find yourself feeling stuck and feel not good enough,

Use a little self-compassion to call that inner critic's bluff.

If you need advice and no one is around, get out a journal,

Pretend your friend needs the same advice, write it out, it's universal.

Tell yourself three things that you love about yourself each day,

Be sincere, and finally, do the things you love, and don't forget to play.

THE CONFIDENT CRONE

When we are younger we sometimes focus on appearance,

Placing far too much value on something that could disappear.

Youth seems immortal as we take it for granted with inexperience

And we flounder about trying to prove we are not oblivious.

Yet, we were oblivious, and there was far too much for us to learn,

In far too short a time, but we would admit we were concerned.

Concerned with everything from how we look to how we dress,

Wanting nothing more than to gain the attention craved and impress.

Not realizing for the longest time, we were trying to fill a void,

Created by grief and trauma, it made us easier to exploit.

Compounding on the past while using it as a weapon for control,

Others would make things worse while pretending to console.

By the time we get wise enough to see through all the games,

And do even more healing work, on whatever remains,

We start to see how vulnerable our rebellious younger self was,

And instead of a facade, we use compassion on our scars.

Your Self-Esteem Free-Writing:

YOUR SELF-ESTEEM FREE-WRITING:

I invite you to join me in a free writing session.

If you have ever struggled with self-esteem, self-worth, or imposter syndrome or have known someone who has, I invite you to do some free writing around that. Try to incorporate three things you truly love about yourself as you write.

Your Self-Esteem Poem(s)

YOUR SELF-ESTEEM POEM(S)

I invite you to read through your free writing and look for any poetry in it. Use it as inspiration to write your own self-worth poems or just let the poetry flow through you.

Learning Love

I misunderstood,
I thought love would complete me,
Just a puzzle piece.

~

Have you ever looked back at what you thought was love and felt your eyes widen in horror? I hope not, but if you did, I am proud of you for learning from those experiences and learning what love really can be for you. I truly believe it comes down to communication and compatibility. As a recovering people pleaser, I had a lot to learn about love. How to communicate my own needs, that it was okay to have those needs, and it was okay to let go of something that wasn't working. It's okay to set it down. Love, real love, should give you more happiness than stress. Real love doesn't make you feel less than your magnificent self. This chapter will have examples of co-dependent love, toxic love, teenage love, and brief fleeting moments of what I thought was real love before I learned to love myself. You will also read a bit about what I've learned through all of that.

DO YOU NOTICE?

As I pull away to prevent myself from hurting,

Do you notice that I am fading away?

As I pull myself away and rebel against co-dependence,

Do you notice that I am suffering?

As I rebel against the hurt that you will bring,

Do you notice I am withering away?

As I close my eyes against the loneliness inside,

Do you notice I need your attention?

As I scream within myself for you to hold me,

Do you notice what you are doing?

As I rebel against the idea of hurt and pain

Do you notice you have made it rain?

As I stand alone in the downpour of emotions,

Do you notice you are not there?

As I cry out in pain while you play your games,

Do you notice that I am leaving today?

THE FLAME OF LOVE

The flame of love,

It reaches to the sky.

The flame of love,

It shines so bright.

One whisper can blow it out,

The flame of love, what's it about?

It starts with caring, and ends with love,

It's as beautiful as a dove.

It takes it slow,

It doesn't rush.

It's cool and calm but burns inside,

The flame of love can't be denied.

CANDLE OF LOVE

Love is pain that burns like a flame,

It grows higher and higher and can't be tamed,

The candle of love has no name.

It can take your soul,

It can take your mind,

Love is pain, it can't be denied.

Love will come,

And love will go,

Try hard not to let it be too close.

Though the tears fall,

Silently from your eyes,

You still try hard not to cry.

The pain takes over,

In your mind, and you feel

As though you should run and hide.

And you promise yourself in your mind,

That you will not ever fall in love,

No, not even one more time

UNFAITHFUL

It can be hard,

Loving someone who's,

Loved so many others.

Loving someone when,

Others will always,

Want to have him.

Sometimes I wish,

You were only mine,

But, I know, the others will be on your mind.

YOU'RE ABOUT TO LEAVE

I'm angry, and I'm sad.

I'm very rarely glad.

I'm needy, and I'm hurting,

And I need you to reassure me.

But you're the reason,

I am feeling all these feelings.

And you can't reassure me,

Because you know you're about to leave.

LEARNING LOVE

Anger and resentment from bitterness and pain,

I cry to the heavens, who do not hear what I say.

Once, I believed in fairy tales, but those days have disappeared,

I fall into the nothingness and emptiness of all my fears.

I cried out in anguish, and the pain was all I felt.

I am bruised and damaged and unable to heal.

If I fall again, I may not survive. I will not live a lie,

But if I love, will I truly live, or will I die?

No, I am not love; I have come to my senses.

I am alone in a world of petty pretenses.

I am alone, different I stand apart.

Born into the emptiness that I feel in my heart.

I cry tears from the heavens rain down,

These people do not know why if they even see my frown.

I long for the love that time will leave me with.

So that I may feel what it is like to have happiness.

LOOKING FOR SOMEONE GOOD

An angel comes to dance at night,

An angel who sees me in a different light.

She's gone away and left me this way,

I had nothing to say; all alone I cried in pain.

No more tears of sorrow, no happiness borrowed,

Freedom lost in pain wishes for the rain.

Death and dying filled my mind,

People leave me if they don't die.

Love is lost, and life is lived,

But no one knows why I'm so listless.

Tired of lies and people who don't try,

I'm just looking for someone good in my life.

LOVE IS

Love is a color both bright and dull.

Love is a flower shining in the sun.

Love is purple, pink, and blue,

Love will linger long after heartbreak.

Love will be there forever somehow, someway.

Love will not fade if it is true.

Love has a way of making you blue.

Love is strong, bold, and free.

Love is a quiet, silent mystery.

Love is forgiving and cannot let go.

Love will remember, and it always knows.

Love knows no secrets or hidden lies.

Love is fiery and does not disguise.

Love is a gift everyone will receive.

Love is patient, and it will wait and see.

Love is quiet, loud, and deaf.

Love can be tricky even to the best.

Love is life and is sacred and pure.

Love is corrupted, and everything blurs.

Love is peaceful, calm, and sweet.

Love is a whisper sweet and serene.

Love is a fairy tale that ends the same.

Love is better than any fame.

Love is something you can't live without.

Love will thrive inside you and out.

MY LOVE

My Love, I love you more than you know.

My Love, I need you so very much.

My Love, I crave you every minute, every hour.

My Love, I yearn for our love to bloom like a flower.

My Love, my everything, I don't want to lose you.

My Love, you're my every being. I hope I'm yours, too.

My Love, my sunrise at the beginning of the day.

My Love, you're simply everything that I might crave.

TOGETHER

We together are like whisper and wind,

Soft and quiet, strong and bold,

You will protect me as I will love you,

We will be together; our love won't grow cold.

You are my life, my inspiration, my hope,

You are my everything I've ever known.

You offer friendship, protection, and love,

You are the light in my life that has barely shown.

I would never dare think,

Of life without you near me,

I can't even begin to think,

Of where or what I'd be.

LOVE I CAN'T HAVE

The kind of love I want,

Is nothing but a song.

The kind of love I dreamed of,

I will never even know.

If I will never have that love,

What sense does it make to live?

Maybe I could fly high above,

Or let go of my dreams of love.

I just can't see why,

I shouldn't want to fly,

I don't want to be around,

For more things to tear me down.

Even my love admits he can't give me,

The kind of love I have always dreamed.

I feel so helpless just thinking of it,

I start to think of things I ought not to think.

LOVE

His love sustains me,

Keeps me here and enraptures me.

His arms hold me safe and secure,

And in them, I am his only girl.

My love for him is overwhelming,

Never would I leave him standing.

This love could last for eternity,

For all the love he gives to me.

Never do I want to see him hurt,

Always, I will know I am his girl.

Forever will my love be true,

This is my love for you.

Love is inconsequential to time,

Your heart knows what rules apply.

Across time and space, my love would go,

To find me safe and hold me close.

Never would he want me to feel alone,

And in his heart, my love, he knows,

Nothing in this world could take him away.

Our love transcends all of reality.

YOU MAKE ME HAPPY

It's funny sometimes that people don't see all the good they do,

Like when you don't see all the happiness, I felt because of you.

There are more times than you know that made me happy inside,

And I think that I should tell you now about some of those times.

When we met, you called me all the time just to tell me you cared,

And when we talked, you listened, and you were always sincere.

For all the times when I wasn't feeling well, and you were there,

And all of the many times that you brushed back or smoothed my hair.

For the day when you told me you would make up for all the bad,

And all the times you held me when I was feeling so very sad.

Especially, for the day you said that you would make me your wife,

I just can't express in words how you have brightened my life.

I was happy each time you wrapped your loving arms around me,

When you held me in your arms just because you loved me and wanted me.

When you told me I was special and beautiful and tried to make me see,

And every single time, we sat or lay together in the dark watching movies.

For all the times I would look at you to find you looking back at me,

And all the times that it seemed that you felt you were lucky to have me,

And all the times you kissed me, and we made love and cuddled,

For all the time you did whatever you could to make me laugh or smile.

I loved that you would listen to me vent, always trying to make me happy,

All the things that you did for me, no expectations because you loved me,

And all the times we did things together, they always made me happy,

There's no way for me to explain the amount of happiness you gave me.

PERHAPS A SOUL MATE

Just two spirits that become one,

Outside the chaos and disorder, they love.

Just two loves across time,

Sharing energy through this life.

I wish for solitude alone with you,

Apart from the chaos of the world, I knew.

Too much drama clouds my space,

I want to scream and turn away.

I long to be away somewhere peaceful,

I retreat into myself deep within my soul.

I looked for you without looking,

I fell for you without falling.

To you, I wish to be a part of for eternity,

Peacefully loving and warm, at last, I feel safety.

Safe and hidden from the pain and anguish,

In your arms, and I feel warmth and happiness.

My smile stays genuine and true around you,

Thoughts of you keep me from the blues.

Everyone must see it, it shows straight through,

They cannot mistake the amount of love I have for you.

WHERE IS MY HEART, WHO AM I?

More than bricks or mortar or siding,

A home is so much more than where you're residing,

A home is where you feel comfort in your heart,

I knew my home was with him from the start.

Within my heart, I felt something warm and new,

And with each kiss we shared and each breath we took,

And at that moment, I found my home, I knew.

I knew that this love was worth all my bad news.

I have lived through many heartaches and many blues,

But I found happiness, comfort, and safety with this one, who,

Took me in with his looks and witty conversation, too,

Made me laugh and was so incredibly sweet and loving, who?

You cannot imagine the joy of feeling so much love,

With the sweets comes the sour, and I had to experience loss,

I lost so much before and lived to be very strong,

But this time the time to heal seemed to take so very long.

I would wake at night from dreams of he and I,

And I never knew if I was supposed to cry,

I would wonder, always, if he dreamed at all of me,

And if someday, perhaps, I could finally be free.

Yes, I must break past the lies and deceit,

I have lied to myself since the day I took my leave,

Always, I thought, we would have another chance at happiness,

But deception was the cause of my self-created prison dance.

I realize now that I must let go soon; this is my plan.

For the one I love, doesn't even know me, I don't think he can.

FOR HIM, I FIGHT

He loved me, even though I was broken,

He saw the light in me when I was fighting the darkness,

He sought to protect me when I was vulnerable,

And he wanted me even when I felt unlovable.

I felt safe within his arms, and it shattered the glass,

Out came all of the darkness from my past,

I wanted to protect him from what once was,

Afraid he wouldn't stay, could he be the one who does?

I wanted to be his light, to burn the darkness away,

I wished to be stronger than ever since that day,

I wanted to be his friend, companion, and warrior,

I wished to make him happy and give him comfort.

He was broken like me in some ways,

Could we help each other move into brighter days?

Or would the darkness swallow one of us up?

All either of us wanted was to find real love.

It wasn't easy for us to open up our hearts,

Sometimes it felt like we were tearing apart,

But we fought through the fog of our pasts,

And our love has kept us together, holding fast.

He doesn't know how far my heart has fallen for him,

And I can't bring myself to believe this could be it.

If I could have a wish, it would be for more laughter,

And for us to finally find we can have that happily ever after.

JUST ME

Your touch, your voice,

Whispers behind me,

My choice.

Walking alone here, my world,

Without love here,

Not heard.

Waking and turning, you'll see,

No more to give here,

Just breath.

Wishing for something, complete,

Not finding someone,

Just me.

Needing affection and love,

Not to confuse you,

With lust.

Seducing spirits, surround,

You left me lonely,

Somehow.

I BELONG TO YOU

*** Awarded the Editor's Choice Award by the International Library of Poetry

I'm scared to love again,

Afraid to lose once more.

Frightened by how I feel for you,

Scared that you'll close the door.

I get lost in my emotions,

Overwhelmed by the things I feel.

Confused about these feelings,

How do I know what is real?

I wish I could explain to you,

Exactly who I really am.

But I don't think you'd see it,

I'm not sure you can.

I have looked for so long,

For someone to treat me right.

Someone to keep me safe,

And someone to hold me tight.

Once you have my heart,

It belongs to only you.

I hope that you understand,

To you, I'll always be true.

SOMEDAY

Gently caress me, hold me, and kiss me.

Whisper like the wind on the sea.

Learn to feel like I feel inside.

These feelings are harder to deny.

Dance with me on the clouds.

We will never touch the ground.

Look into my eyes and truly see.

See me when I feel I can truly be.

Long forgotten fairytales remembered.

Will all my dreams be surrendered?

Will someone save me from my doubts?

Someday I will know what love is about.

TRUE LOVE?

*** Awarded the Editor's Choice Award by the International Library of Poetry

I am dreaming of a love that even time will leave alone,

And in the darkness of the night together we will hold,

And from the good times to the bad, we stay true and loyal,

And he will let me know that for him there is no other.

I am dreaming of a love that I fear does not exist,

I fear there is no one else who loves me quite like this,

Deep within my heart, I can only hope and pray,

That I will find someone who can love me the same way.

I am dreaming of someone who can love me like I love them,

Someone who will never shy away from holding my hand,

Someone who is willing to wipe away all my tears,

And someone with whom I can spend the rest of all my years.

I am dreaming of a love that I know is very rare,

In their time of madness, it seems everyone despairs,

But I will stay true to myself and give all my heart,

I can only hope I will find someone who won't tear it apart.

CAN HE SEE

Can he see me through the shadows?

Will he accept me for who I am?

Many things in life you will not understand.

Can he save me from the darkness?

How do I know if he even wants to try?

Will he wipe away the tears that I cry?

Can you see me through the darkness?

Can I let someone else in?

Strange how I may need this thing.

Strange how this surprised me.

These feelings and these thoughts.

Against these very things, I have fought.

Will this leave me broken,

Or is it more than it seems?

Perhaps it is less, an empty dream.

These silly thoughts mean nothing,

It's impossible for me to fall.

I have no intentions, none at all.

LEARNING ABOUT LOVE

Love can be wonderful

And fill you with joy,

If the one you love,

Loves you more than a toy.

I'm sad to say it happens,

That's the way with some,

They want to please,

Themselves and you're not their only one

If you are lucky and

You find a man who,

Treats you like gold,

Keep him forever, and never let go.

He'll tell you he loves you,

He'll show the whole world,

He'll be with only you,

And you'll know his love is true.

Love can take. a while,

To grow strong and trust,

But when you start to,

Feel it, your heart just might bust.

SO DAMN HARD TO LOVE

I am trapped in the darkness,

Lost deep within the shadows.

I am hanging in limbo,

Waiting for your song.

I am waiting for a dance with you,

Wondering what I would do.

Thinking if I should or should not,

Let you deep within.

But there is something in your eyes,

That makes it hard to open up.

There is something in your heart,

That makes you so damn hard to love.

There is something stopping me,

From letting you in completely.

There is something that I need,

That you can't give to me.

There is something in the shelter,

That you provide for me.

That makes me want to love you,

Then I knew it couldn't be.

NEVER LOVE

I need a love that can see me,

Someone to give what I can give.

I need to know that I am seen,

I need a love that's my fantasy.

Instead of thinking of love is lost,

Instead of wishing you had some other,

Listening to reminders of what you had,

Maybe you could love me tonight Instead.

LOVE SONGS

These love songs are empty promises,

Or reminders of what I can never have.

Constant reminders of what could be,

Of something that they can have, but not me.

I listen, and I understand all the words.

I feel all of the emotions of the song.

But will someone ever feel that way for me?

Is there a forever kind of love that I see?

The love that I need is nothing but a song.

Not meant to come true. It's all wrong.

There was supposed to be a song for me.

Something that said someone loved me for me.

Instead, I hear all the words and feel alone,

Maybe there is still someone to love me after all.

Someone who can say these songs are for me,

Is there a chance these songs can truly be?

Love seems to be scarce these days in my world,

Maybe I can't have someone who doesn't think of her.

It is possible that one love outlasts the next,

While I give all my heart to feel like I'm second best.

A WISH

I sit by the water, searching for love.

I sit by the water, searching the skies above.

My life it seems is not meant for these feelings.

In my life, it seems, that love is not meant to be.

I wished on a star, one moonlight glowing night,

That love would come to find me, a love that is right.

Kisses, soft caresses, a passionate fire inside,

A love that accepts me. There is no need to hide.

I dreamt of a love that made me feel whole,

With beauty and comfort, I long to behold.

It wraps around me and protects me from harm,

I know that I am safe, I feel it in his arms.

AS I SIT

As I sit here, and I wonder,

Why did I fall again?

I think about the promises,

To never need anyone again.

As I sit here, I wonder,

When will you break my heart?

I did not want to fall,

But I did not want to part.

As I sit here, I wonder,

Why you had to be you?

Because I absolutely adore you,

But still, I did not want to fall.

As I sit here, I wonder,

Why I think of you all day,

I did not want to fall,

But I couldn't bear to be away.

As I sit here, I wonder,

When will you hurt me?

I know it will happen. It has to be,

Because I didn't want to fall so easily.

As I sit here, I wonder,

How I fell from my place.

For I was a star unreachable,

Until I saw love in your face.

WILL SHE?

*** Awarded the Editor's Choice Award by the International Library of Poetry

She's been hurt and torn and left broken,

Told that nothing good will ever happen,

She's cried and screamed and died inside,

Still, there are things she can't deny.

Will fear run through her from this point on,

Will her life become just another sad song,

Or can she take the chance and let things go,

Will she or won't she let him know?

It's strange to her, these feelings she has,

Somehow, she no longer feels so sad,

This should be good, to be happy so often

But she's scared of what will happen

Yes. she's happy, and she smiles, it's nice

But what happens when he's cold as ice,

Or one day, when it all starts to change,

Maybe she can't think about that day.

Brokenhearted too many times before,

She just keeps looking at the door,

Wondering how she let someone in,

Does he realize what she feels for him?

LET GO

Holding back these feelings,

Holding back these thoughts,

Holding back these things inside,

I just can't let myself be caught.

Holding on to nothing special,

Holding on to someone dear,

Holding on to painful memories,

I just can't let someone near.

Letting go of all the bad things,

Letting go of all my tears,

Letting go of painful memories,

I need someone to hold me here.

Trying to move on from all these things,

Trying to find true love,

Trying to let go of ghosts,

I have to let go. I have just begun.

KISSES, FLOWERS AND ROMANCE

*** Awarded the Editor's Choice Award by the International Library of Poetry

I had dreams of kisses and passion,

Of flowers and dancing leaves,

Romance, fairy tales and love,

The moonlit sky is just out of reach.

I still see a night so beautiful,

Gone into the darkness, it was born.

I still feel the caress across my face,

But the caress and kisses are gone.

Still searching for that romance,

Believing in that fairy-tale love,

Waiting for you to show me,

Needing to feel your touch.

NO MORE FAIRY TALE

I think the love I had always dreamed of simply does not exist,

I had hoped that I had found it through every relationship,

Searching for that which I thought could bring happiness,

I found hopelessness, thoughtlessness, and profound sadness.

I thought that I could find another with ideals like mine.

I thought there could be someone that was of a similar mind,

Someone who could be faithful and love me unconditionally,

Someone who believed in love and who could believe in me.

Too many times, I tried to see what was not really there,

Trying to believe in something that was as thin as the air,

Trying to create a relationship that could be considered fair,

Foolish enough to continue believing in my own fairy tale.

THINGS I LOVE

I love the way you make me laugh,

And the way you make me forget the past,

I love the looks and smiles you have,

And did I mention how you make me laugh?

I love that you can make me laugh when I'm mad,

And sometimes you make me laugh when I'm sad,

I love all of the crazy moments we have had,

I do think that the good outweighs the bad.

I hope one day that you can feel my love,

And I hope one day that you can return that love,

I hope one day I can be all that you need,

And one day, I hope you really know me.

WHO I DREAM TO BE

I am a beautiful person, and I strive to be a beautiful person,

I dream of a love that never dies and always tries,

I am a strong person who sometimes gets lost in someone else,

I dream of a person I can get lost in, that can return me.

I am a loving person, and I strive to take care of myself, but be unselfish,

I dream of a time when people all have a sense of honor,

I am an Empathic person, and I strive to help those that I may,

I dream of a person so in tune with me that I don't need to explain.

I am a creative and open-minded person; I strive to maintain that outlook,

I dream of a love that is clear for the whole world to see,

I am a spiritual being; I strive to be positive, calm, and happy,

I dream of a person that brings out the best in me.

I am an intelligent person; I strive to balance intelligence with intuition,

I dream of a romance that is full of pleasant surprises and love,

I'm simply different in many good ways, trying not to be anything negative,

I dream of a life where I am respected and accepted just for me.

CONFUSED

He said I love you,

She said he's no good.

He said don't listen,

I said I'm confused.

I love her kisses,

Her skin feels so soft.

He makes me shiver,

Knocks my game off.

I have to choose now,

Which way do I go?

They tell me one way,

But I'm not so sure.

It makes them uneasy,

My attraction to her.

It makes it appealing,

To rebel and be heard.

I'm so confused now,

Which way do I turn?

With the passion increasing,

I fear I'll be burned.

LOVE OR LUST

Against the wall, heart beating faster,

This will be love, or this will be a disaster.

Lust and love are similar, this is which one?

Can I stop the emotion to make sense long enough?

PERFECT IMPERFECT LOVE

He will hold me like he never wants to let go,

Never doubts that with me, he wants to grow old,

As he brushes back my hair and caresses my face,

Always I will know that in his heart, I have a place

He will listen to my heart when it speaks to him,

And no matter the distance, he knows I will be his.

He will make me smile even through my sadness,

And I will give everything to shelter him from the madness.

I will give him all of my heart without hesitation,

And never take for granted our time or occasion.

I will dance for him and hold him close when he desires,

And never wander from our love, loyalty, and fire.

I will never need doubt that his heart will be eternally mine,

For when we look at each other we see it in our eyes.

Some will say our love doesn't exist or belong in this world,

But it is here, perfect in its' imperfection, our love will be born.

I wonder where it is that I should fit into this lunacy,

They don't want one true love. It seems they prefer at least three.

Is my soul too old for this new digitally charged world?

All of this has left my heart and soul more than knurled.

Still, I am a stubborn bull, or maybe I am the mule,

Because I keep searching for a rare jewel, like a fool.

I wonder if anyone, at all, still feels as I do now,

Or have they all found their match, and I'm the odd one out.

It's enough that I question if I should wait at all,

Two years and counting without the touch of love.

So, I am antiquated because I will not give myself away,

Not until I find a love, a singular love, that I'm sure will stay.

MISSED LOVE

I thought love was forever and I was wrong,

I loved you so much and now you are gone.

You tell me that I didn't do anything wrong,

You just can't stay with someone that long.

You told me that you didn't know it would be this hard,

So, after two years, you tell me we should part.

I thought we could work it out, but you shook your head,

To every solution that I could have possibly said.

I wonder to this day the real reason that you left,

Because you never gave an answer to satisfy my head.

I wonder was there someone else or just your friends & games,

It hurts me more to think that I came second to a video game.

NO ONE LOVES ME LIKE HE DOES

Independent in isolation, ignored,

I gave you my heart. Do I have yours?

Lost, lonely, lingering loss,

How much sorrow death has caused?

Alone, afraid, abandoned, and angry,

I wanted someone to take care of me.

Silent Solitude secrets, so serene,

Hold me, love me, and always protect me.

Life, longer lasting for love,

No one loves me like he does.

SCARED TO DEATH OF LOVE

Love takes time to heal old wounds,

You left me in a world so cruel,

What was it I was here to do?

I really can't remember. Maybe you do.

Silently, I remember many old dreams,

Though I'm not sure what any of it means.

Happy, I am, that I fell in love,

But scared to death of it all, scared to death of love.

SEARCHING FOR WHO

I feel myself pulling slowly away,

Withdrawing deep within myself,

There is no real reason for me to stay,

I find there is no one left to help.

I struggle within the depths of my heart,

To let go and be whole once more,

But again, I am reminded of being torn,

And my mind whispers insidiously love is war.

There is no such thing as an eternal love,

I could cry out to the heavens and rise above,

I know loyalty is simply just a false emotion,

Sometimes, I wish I were a part of the ocean.

If loyalty were real, it'd be body, mind and soul,

But too often, I have seen that this is not so,

Many seek, through others, to fill the hole,

So, from bar to bar and person to person, they go.

I have no more delusions that love can be true,

My heart would be torn apart by his desire for something new,

If I gave my heart again, deception would rule,

Still, forever, my heart is searching, but I ask for who.

LAST CHANCE

I once had true love, but it left me cold,

Now, I have chosen to live forever alone,

I gave my true love the last of my heart,

But he walked out on me and tore it all apart.

I once had my soul mate to hold me tight,

But things got too hard for him, and he took flight,

I thought this time was different. I felt his love,

But in the end, he was gone, like almost everyone.

I once had a love that I felt loved me back,

But sadly, he seemed to want his lonely life back,

I feel so hurt and so very alone, but this is the end,

I will not ever allow myself to fall in love again.

WILL YOU COME BACK

I often ask myself if and when you might come back,

But the more time that goes by, the more I wonder if it's me you lack.

I often think about you at night before I go to sleep,

And I wonder if, when you lay down, you think of me?

You said you loved me, and you just needed some space,

But I wonder if there is more behind the sad look upon your face.

You can point out all the petty things I do wrong,

But in the end, you will think about the love missing from your arms.

You can tell me that you love me, but then throw it all away,

So, if you come back, I just won't know if you will stay.

Now I sit here wondering just what it is that I should do,

Because, the love I have inside, well, it's all there for you.

Now I know what it is that I really want from love,

I want someone who will treat me like I'm as precious as a dove,

And someone to fight for me and hold me tight at night,

Someone who knows there are always troubles in life.

I need someone who understands they cannot just walk away,

Just because times are rough and their reserves are starting to sway,

Someone who will be strong, and I'll know will be there to stay,

Someone who loves me as I am, simply because I am just that way.

LOST LOVE

With love, there must come pain,

And sometimes happiness brings the rain.

Even when your heart is broken,

Your wounds will heal, and doors will open.

When true loves become heartbreakers,

Your heart grows strong against all takers.

Time will heal all your wounds,

And to be alone, you can still choose.

Lost in a world you perceive as cruel,

You still think about a love so true.

But too often, you have been left behind,

And to try again, you feel, is most unkind.

I have felt a love that felt true and right,

But in the end, it was simply a fight.

He left me alone, heart and soul,

And it left my heart feeling cold.

See what happens when I give love a chance,

I end up being betrayed and hurt again.

Still, I know my wounds will someday heal,

And perhaps someday I can learn again to feel.

MURDEROUS LOVE

I staggered, broken,

His murderous love,

He can see me crying.

Not together, I whisper,

And fall against my knees.

A KISS

All I wanted was a kiss,

But a kiss from him would never come,

He hides in the shadows of the pieces of someone,

Afraid to step out and hold something whole.

All I wanted was a kiss,

But for that, I would have to let him in,

And I never chase. In fact, I often run away,

Afraid to let anyone in because they might shatter me.

All I wanted was a kiss,

But for her, it might mean more,

And I wouldn't want to hurt or disappoint her,

So, I am frozen with indecision, lacking the liquid courage.

All I wanted was a kiss,

But with him, it was disappointing,

Soul mate he may once have been but no more,

He cut me so deeply I couldn't open my heart's door.

All I wanted was a kiss,

But I cannot kiss just anyone,

No, I must have a connection and feelings,

And it must be fun and with someone I trust.

All I wanted was a kiss,

But not just any kiss would do,

No, I wanted a heart-racing, breathtaking sensation,

A kiss where you pause to savor and slowly go in for more.

All I wanted was a kiss,

Full of passion, desire, and even love,

One that makes me want so much more than just that,

But to have this kiss, first I must find that someone.

AN ANTIQUATED DESIRE

Is it this antiquated notion of a monogamous, singular love,

The very thing that will have me come undone?

Lost in the sea of all the plenty going fishing,

Is it any wonder that Cupid's arrows keep missing?

Searching through a quagmire of faces and words,

Harmony is not found among these massive herds.

Make the decision, and make it as quick,

Make it based on things that are baseless.

I'm sorry, did you want something of substance?

Not here, not now in this time of digital madness.

In my twenties, often I did, confuse lust with love,

Giving my heart completely to my quickly rising pulse.

Now, it seems the majority is to follow suit,

They troll the unknown, looking for what, not who.

Where once I sought him, my true loves embrace,

And believed with all my heart there was such a thing as fate.

Now, I watch the trolling antics of the digitally lost,

Hungry for their self-centered desires regardless of the cost.

I suppose they do not know what it is they really gave up,

This is a disposable society. This is the life to which they are accustomed.

Don't like what you've tasted? Just toss it to the side,

There will always be someone else you can take for a ride.

IT'S REAL, IT'S LOVE

I could write you a poem of sunshine and rainbows,

And I could tell you only all the things I love about you,

But I think it would be, somehow less to you, insincere,

Because part of what makes us beautiful is wrapped in tears.

I love you for all the wonderful pieces of you that I see,

But I also love you for the ways that you challenge me,

I want to, and do, love you even more for all your broken pieces,

And for each crack in your armor, I'd mend it with pieces of me.

I've never had a love like this that I recall in my entire life,

The way you already talk about maybe making me your wife,

It fills me with fear, I admit, but also joy and excitement,

It seems so fast, and yet so long, but maybe that means it's right.

You might not know, but I see the sun shine through your eyes,

And it's been a really long time since I let someone hold me as I cry,

For as long as I can remember, I had to be independent and strong,

And I love that you encourage that, but give me a shoulder to cry on.

I love the way you see through me, that you care enough to see,

Although sometimes I wish you didn't so I could protect you from me,

I never want to hurt you. I want to make you feel happy and safe,

I think it's sad that sometimes you think you don't deserve to be saved.

I especially love the way you will apologize when you are wrong,

And the way you try to stop me from tearing myself completely apart,

Even when you're angry, even when you hurt, you think of how I feel,

And I've never had that in all my memories of living here.

Sometimes I get scared, sometimes I'm fighting demons I can't share,

It's never because I don't want to, and it's almost always because I care,

I fight them alone to save you, to save me, but mostly to save us,

Because that is what you need, and I promise to try to never give up.

I love that you are in touch with your emotions, that you embrace feelings,

And sometimes it makes me crazy when you can't handle feelings from me,

I love to see you struggle to stay calm. I see it in your face and your eyes,

Because it means you fought demons and won, so you wouldn't see me cry.

I've never had anyone fight in any way for me, and you do it in many ways,

I love that you can hold me, look me in the eyes, and make me feel safe,

I fall in love with you all over again when you caress my face.

I've had moments where I wished we could shut the world out for days.

I even love the way you get scared for me and even sometimes insecure,

It's oddly comforting to know someone is afraid that I'll get hurt,

And on the other hand, it means you feel you have something to lose,

If something were to happen to me, I'd fight to the death to protect you.

I love that you are thoughtful and considerate the way that I once was,

And that you've awakened a part of me that I thought was long past gone,

I hate that I don't feel good enough, and I hate when I have doubts,

But I love that we've been real enough to let that air out.

I love that you teach me ways to be safe, and show me ways to act,

In this way, you give me some of my own personal power back.

I wish we had more time, for myself and to make you feel better too,

But I know we will have more time. We will make more time soon.

I love that you inspire me to be the best version of myself,

And I hope I do that for you because, to me, that is what love is about.

I love that you encourage me and push me towards my dreams,

Although I've come to care so much for you, it's harder for me to sing,

I feel like a flower must feel, one that didn't bloom with all the rest,

One who started to think she'd never open up or ever be the best.

Then, one day, she sees the sun, and it shines on her so warm and bright,

She starts to slowly unfold. You are my sun. I see it in your eyes.

I love all your surprises. That shows me how much you think of me,

And I get frustrated that for you, I cannot seem to do the same thing,

But I look forward to the day when I can fully express to you my love,

I promise you, there is so much that I will give when I really open up.

V-DAY

If I could, I would grant you one wish,

I would grant you my openness.

It's not an easy road to travel, and it might make you sore,

But if you can make it through to the end, you will know my heart is yours.

Despite the fear that wells up inside me,

At the idea of sharing unpleasant thoughts and memories,

I will let you past the walls once more,

And once again, I chose to let you open my heart's door.

For I have thrown my walls back up quite by accident,

Trying to be what you needed, trying to prove I could move past all of it.

It, being the selfish tendencies that I have seen,

When you're unsure of your emotions, stressed, and can't stop being mean.

It, being the despair, you felt but could not identify,

Forcing me to watch my positivity die.

It, being that overwhelming feeling of loss.

When I finally realized I had a partner, he was gone.

It, being the struggle, I felt every day for months as I again came second.

To the one person, I thought would never make me feel abandoned.

It, being the fear that keeps me silent, even when you ask what is wrong.

Because you ask but I doubt that you really want to know what's going on.

It, being the fear that I am too broken for anyone to really love,

Or the fear that the love I want is nothing but made up.

It, being the fear that I will never see myself as good enough,

It's so easy to see your criticisms as proof and I just sort of come undone.

It, being the fear that telling you any of this at all,

Will be the very thing that results in our relationship's downfall.

But here I am writing you this tragic poem,

Not to make you feel bad, but to allow you to see inside my storm,

Telling you about all the pain I feel knowing you might not understand.

Because doubts, pain, and troubles aside I don't want any other man.

I LOVE YOU

I love you,

I needed you to know that.

I love you with more in my heart than I imagined I could have.

I love you,

For the way you never give up.

I love you for all the ways you make me feel loved.

I love you,

These three words used so commonly,

And tossed about and rarely associated logically.

I love you,

I chose you, an honor you couldn't understand,

Logically weighing my emotions and carefully extending my hand.

I love you,

Because I saw you as strong and gentle,

These two qualities, seemingly opposites, were to me, complemental.

I love you,

For the way, I can see the sun in your eyes,

The way the warmth of your gaze penetrates my difficult & hardened guise.

I love you,

Despite the difficult road we have traveled,

Because you fought to stop our love from being completely unraveled.

I love you,

In ways, words can never fully express,

From the look in your eyes, to the soft caress on my skin or your kiss on my lips.

I love you.

I needed you to know,

Because I'm learning love needs two people willing to feed it and help it grow.

YOUR DOG TAGS

I sleep with your dog tags in my hand some nights,

I hold it close to my heart because it's the only piece of you I have to hold.

So even when you're not here sometimes you protect me from my demons,

Just holding that small piece of you seems to help me past that fright,

Your dog tags make things feel alright.

THE BEST KIND OF LOVE

Soft whispers and sweet caresses,

Remind one another who they are with.

They will never lie,

Or say goodbye,

They will understand,

And never demand.

They will care,

And always be there,

They will not separate,

Or be subject to great heartache,

They will not get loud,

Or jump all about,

They will not fight.

They will be alright.

They will always come home,

And never leave another alone.

They will listen and be patient,

And when something is wrong, they'll fix it.

They will not put each other down,

Or make the other look at the ground.

They are in love, the best kind of love around.

PUSH AND PULL

It's like a perpetual push and pull,

Sometimes it is them, and sometimes it's me,

Too far away, and not too close,

That is where things seem to need to be.

I've had love that pushed and pulled,

Too many times for me to trust it,

To close and you push, too far and you pull,

You can't let me in and once again I'm hurt.

I've had a love that I pushed and pulled,

Pushed to feel, pulled back to be safe,

Because of the others before I learned

Too close and I'd run, run fast and far away.

Some really want to fight the war in my heart,

I've had them ask me, what I have to say,

How can I make you see it can be different?

I'd say it's not words, it's your actions, just stay.

But those words ring hollow as I close my heart,

To the many games that so many play,

It happens all the time, and I am aware,

I make it exceptionally difficult for someone to stay.

I have frightened myself at the intensity I feel,

I couldn't fault another for succumbing to fear,

Then in my mind, I've justified they will succumb,

And I've decided it's no longer safe for me here.

At times I worry about the people I love,

I'll run, I'll fly, I'll walk far away from it all,

Because I don't want to hurt them, I'll leave,

Building myself an even larger stronger wall.

I've been afraid to love for so very long,

The idea of it has become foreign to me now,

I'm not sure I would know it, not for sure,

Maybe it's been so long that I forgot how.

I LOVED

I loved you when we met.

I loved you when we dated.

I loved you when we lived together.

I loved you even when I hated.

I loved you with a broken heart.

I loved you when you were gone.

I loved you when you were close.

I loved you when you were lost.

I loved you enough to be there.

I loved you enough to let go.

I loved you enough to move on.

I loved you enough to not let you know.

I loved the way you held me close.

I loved the way you made me laugh.

I loved the way I knew just by your look.

I loved the way you took away the sadness.

I love that I can always look back.

I love that I can take this with me.

I love that you have set new standards.

I love that I know it can once more be.

I love that I can move into the future.

I love that I have learned so much.

I love that someday someone will come.

I love that on that day I can take this and move on.

YOUR EYES

I'm just sitting here waiting for a message on the phone,

I'm thinking about how your eyes feel like home.

Like a sunset in the mountains on a fall day,

Or, like high noon in the summer as the trees sway.

LOVE'S DESPAIR

It seems love can push you to limits,

That you never could have reached before.

It can make you happier than ever,

Or it can leave you dying on the floor.

It can leave you feeling whole again,

Or it can break you into pieces.

It can build you up or tear you down,

And offer the ultimate of releases.

LET GO OR STAY

I have written songs for you and cried for you.

I have agonized over conflicting feelings for you.

I have hoped for you, loved you, and hated you.

I have wanted to be with and away from you.

A GIFT

Love is a precious gift,

Sometimes misunderstood,

But when truly found,

It can make everything good.

TOXICITY

It wasn't you.

It wasn't me.

It was us, this wasn't meant to be.

The blame is yours,

The blame is mine,

We couldn't make it work this time.

I damaged you,

You damaged me,

Fighting against our incompatibility.

LEARNING LOVE AS THE MAIDEN

She just wanted to love with her whole heart,

She wanted that soul mate that would never part,

She was searching for that, *you complete me moment,*

Her only references to a happy love were movie moments.

Coming from a broken home, with even more broken parents,

She faltered quite a bit, and she was far too transparent.

She wouldn't have guessed putting it all out there was dangerous,

But she was ever naive and prone to granting immediate trust.

So, the vicious circle began when she was too small to remember,

Exposed to men with wandering hands and unpredictable tempers,

Deep in her subconscious were the lessons that she unwittingly learned.

And as she grew older, they would inevitably return.

The unknown forces driving her to men that perpetuated misuse,

And her naive nature made it easy for others to resort to abuse.

Her blind trust presented larger problems with time,

As she would end up in situations not realizing the lies.

The cycle in her heart and mind, are more clear with reflection,

It all started with falling head over heels for someone unhealthy.

Then she would start to feel disenchanted, abused, or lonely,

Wondering what she had done to cause them to behave remotely.

It wasn't all on them, she had some self-sabotaging behavior,

And let's not forget the pattern of picking unhealthy strangers,

She didn't realize she was setting herself up for failure,

Instead excusing their treatment convinced she was their savior.

When things were good, they were great, her emotions were high,

But she didn't know anything about the triggers from her past life,

And when it was bad it drove her down into the darkest emotions,

That would be one of her self-esteem's greatest erosions.

She saw herself as the victim and she saw life as unfair,

With everything she'd been through she just wanted love to share.

She didn't realize she had to love herself completely first,

Perhaps if she had one of the relationships might have worked.

LEARNING LOVE AS THE MOTHER

Once you become a mother or move beyond the maiden phase,

You begin to become intolerant, of once-acceptable ways.

Finding yourself through healing a little more each day,

Things that once bound you to someone no longer have sway.

You start to see the pattern in the decisions and choices you made,

And you begin to understand, that for love, there are many ways.

There comes an understanding that it's more about compatibility,

And control is not anywhere near the same thing as stability.

You hold yourself accountable for all your imperfections, true,

But you begin to hold others responsible for their action too.

Still, you might struggle with incompatible love a little longer,

Believing perhaps, you can save them with the love you have to offer.

Sometimes, you'll stay for the kids, they need a father and a mother,

Convinced they're better off if you fill the absent seat with another.

You become aware this might be another thing from which to recover.

Yet, you know now, that you have grown to be much tougher.

You start to break from loves that fall short of what you deserve.

And you start to put real value on those that make you feel heard.

As you grow to love yourself and heal yourself more,

Relationships grow or wither, not able to be what they were before.

Though you may or may not see it in the moment that it happens,

You are growing your relationships and improving your interactions.

Soon you will be able to confidently love and trust with ease,

As you fully embrace your newly acquired expertise.

LEARNING LOVE AS THE CRONE

You have traveled from the naivety of the maiden,

Moving through the jaded mother's expectations,

You've found yourself no longer looking for love outside,

Finding it within became the greatest prize.

There is no need for someone to complete you,

You, my dear, are complete as you journey through,

Completed, as in whole, even when you feel the void,

You, are exquisite even when you feel utterly destroyed.

Your value doesn't come from the love of others,

Proof that you are lovable doesn't come from the number of lovers,

You know this, you can feel inside, you are so much more,

This time YOU are the person you desire to explore.

Your Love Lessons Free-Writing:

YOUR LOVE LESSONS FREE-WRITING:

I invite you to join me in a free writing session.

There is so much we could write about when it comes to love, from lessons learned to the love of your dreams. Write about your reflections on love or the love you dream of having.

Your Love Poem(s)

YOUR LOVE POEM(S)

Take a moment to read through your free writing and look for any poetry in it. Use it as inspiration to write your own love poems or just let the poetry flow through you. Sometimes circling words that rhyme can help you see patterns.

Natures Wonder

As the ice coats it,
Beautifully shimmering,
A wonderland tree.

~

I have often sought refuge, solace, and healing in nature. Some of these poems will be very old (or young), depending on your perspective, but all the poetry within this chapter is about nature. Many studies that show the benefits of nature. From a long walk in a wooded area to gardening in your backyard. Time in nature helps reduce stress and supports hormones, blood pressure, and feelings of isolation. Some studies show it can increase mood and beneficial cells that help the immune system. So, when you are feeling down or unwell, try a walk in nature, sit in nature, or both! I recently found real value, peace and grounding in simply stepping outside and planting my bare feet in the grass or soil. I reveal in feeling the soft caress of the wind on my skin or rippling through my hair. In the summer I enjoy feeling the sun kissing my skin beaconing the freckles to rise to the surface. I hope you stop and see the magic of a passing dragonfly, butterfly, rabbit or bird.

SKY

Purple and pink are the colors I see,

In the beautiful sky that looks like the sea.

In the daytime, it glows a bright blue-green,

In the nighttime, it changes color naturally.

I can see the birds fly high into the clouds,

And I sometimes wonder why nothing seems loud.

Careful I am when I start to wish,

I wish I could fly or maybe swim like a fish.

I could fly higher and higher through the sky,

Until no one could see me with the naked eye.

I wouldn't harm anyone if left alone,

When things get hard, I wish I had flown.

CASTLE IN THE SKY

I want to live in a faraway land,

I want to see the beautiful sand.

I want to find a true love that cares,

I want someone I know will always be there.

I want all of my dreams to come true,

I want to take a walk through the beautiful woods.

I want a castle in the sky, where I can fly so very high,

I want a castle in the sky that would be forever mine.

I want a world filled with peace, not war,

I don't want to see any more blood on a sword.

I want music, laughter, dancing, and joy you can't buy,

I want to watch birds fly by, up in my castle in the sky.

THE WEEPING WILLOW

Why does a weeping willow weep?

Is it because the sadness is too sweet?

Why does it hang its leaves like I hang my head?

Why can't I sleep in the depths of my bed?

Does it feel the hurt of the world around,

Or is it gravity that pulls it down?

Why does a weeping willow weep?

Is it because it can't sleep?

It lies awake to see so much pain,

Or is it because the sky fills with rain?

Why does a weeping willow weep?

If only it could answer me.

SAVE THE TREES

*** As first published in rhythms a college literary magazine

The trees sway against the howling wind.

They shake and twist but refuse to bend.

The rainfall comes and pounds the trees,
But they stand tall and look to me.

The sun beats down on the trees by my side,

As if to fade them away to sad goodbyes.

The snow pours down and covers the trees,

As if to smother them, yet it smothers me.

The trees stand tall and still right now,

As I give them my life and then lie down.

The trees stand tall, but reach for me,

They give me the strength that I need.

They bring me back to life, you see;

So, I ask you all, please save the trees.

NATURE FRIENDS

Sorry to leave you on such short notice,

But the reason I left was strictly business.

I had a job that I had to do,

It really has nothing to do with you.

I'm leaving again tomorrow as well,

I'm leaving again, but I wish you well.

I have a trip that I must take,

A trip that goes down along the lake.

The lake, the sea, and the ocean too,

If I could, I wouldn't doubt taking you.

The trees they help me, make up my thoughts,

The air tells me things that are never taught.

So, I'm sorry to leave on so short a time,

But I have to go and visit a friend of mine.

OUR MOTHER

Through the forest and down the stream,

You realize what nature is coming to be.

Beautiful and free, until we came around,

Now, everyone wants to tear her to the ground.

Our mother, who takes us in and gives us everything,

We dishonor, violate her, and don't care about anything.

Without the earth, we would cease to exist,

But that doesn't seem to matter to those feeling less.

Soon, they will starve or burn in the sun alive,

After their defeat, all of nature will once again thrive.

THE UNIVERSE

The moon floats,

The rain hopes,

The stars wait,

Heaven in peace,

In northern lights,

Curves planets to look.

THE SAND AND THE OCEAN

The sand and the ocean work together as partners.

The sand and the ocean have respect for one another.

The sand and the ocean, the rocks and the twigs.

The sand and the ocean know almost everything.

The sand is hot and does not cool until night,

The ocean is cold but warm deep inside.

The ocean is cool, calm, and collected,

The sand is rough, hot, and objective.

The sand and the ocean, the ocean and the sand.

They hold a certain spot for a certain kind of man.

TO BE A STAR

I wonder if the stars feel,

The pressure of the black hole,

Do they feel suffocated by the darkness,

That is their home?

They light up the sky and inspire us with so much hope,

Even as they die,

Shooting across the sky,

Offering us wishes to cope.

I wonder if they ever feel,

They are drowning in the darkness,

Looking to the sun for comfort,

But not able to ask for it.

I wonder if they find comfort,

In the moon's soft glow, like I do,

And on better days does the darkness of the night,

Sometimes feel like a cocoon.

I wonder if they get lonely up there all alone,

Looking down at us,

Shining every night as we look up,

And smile at them. Are they conscious?

WHERE I BELONG

I am a creature filled with love for this earth,

No matter what goes on, someone will always be hurt.

It is at this time that they realize their own mortality,

And hopefully, they see that they can be eternally happy.

No matter what the cause of their pain, their wounds can heal,

And no matter how hard it rains, at least, you can still feel.

I feel the raindrops on my skin, and it feels like a piece of heaven.

I feel the earth beneath my toes, and I once again feel whole.

I long to see the moonlight staring down upon my face.

Bathing in the moonlight I have some kind of faith,

And in the darkness wrapped within its deepest folds.

I find, I can still seek out my sanity and grab a hold.

Under the starry night when the stars are shining so bright.

I feel so beautiful and know that my eyes shine just as bright.

As the wind blows through my hair while I walk along the shore.

I feel I have everything I ever needed, and I need no more.

When I travel through the woodlands and disappear into the trees.

I know in my heart that there is no other place meant for me.

SNOW

What a wonderland was created in this wintery bluster,

As the ice coats the trees and the snowfall becomes a buffer,

A natural soundproofing insulation from the outside world

That I cheerfully toast my tea, as I give it a little stir.

Wrapped in my own cocoon of blankets, watching a fireplace roar,

With a stack of books beside me, I could hardly ask for more,

No one will come calling for me to leave my sanctuary,

This is just another of nature's little gifts to me.

While others see hazardous roads too slick to travel,

I see beauty in the snow falling like a cotton ball unraveled,

And each snowflake in its own pristine, complete uniqueness,

Serves as a reminder of our own unique completeness.

We are simply as that snowflake is, perfect in all its beauty.

Sharing ourselves with the world is our ultimate duty,

Landing softly on the trees with others similar but never the same,

Collectively insulating the soil protecting it once again.

A nuisance to those who don't understand its purpose,

It protects the roots of all the trees by covering the surface.

Regulating the temperature of this beautiful green planet,

It's a symbol of transformation as well if you can believe it.

In the springs, when the snow slowly recedes and disappears,

I take comfort knowing it has returned to reservoirs and rivers,

Representing a cycle of life, transformation, and rebirth,

I look forward every year now, to watching the snow coat the earth.

WATERFALLS

They needn't be very tall,

The magic is present if they are small,

The babbling sounds of the water over stones,

Carries through the woods from here to the unknown.

The sound of the waterfalls brings a sense of peace,

And a safe place for pain to be released,

Supported as always by the surrounding trees,

As they speak to you softly, carrying on the breeze.

If it's warm enough, you can dip your toes into the stream,

Or find small pockets at the bottom to swim and enjoy the scene,

Some will run and jump from the tippy top,

While others watch from the bottom as they drop.

I find the more isolated spots to be the best,

It provides me solitude and a different kind of rest,

A rest that carries through deep down in my bones,

And offers so much more to my weary soul.

I always come away with a sense of rejuvenation,

That can only come from a deeper form of relaxation,

Ultimately, gifting me with an unparalleled sense of liberation.

Spending this time in nature is simply a natural deep meditation.

IRELAND

Oh, Island of Erie,

How you felt like home,

As I sat atop of Knowth,

I felt a connection I'd never known.

And o'er at the Cliffs of Moher,

I felt happiness hit my soul,

At the precipice, I watched the waves crash ashore,

And stood in awe, watching birds soar.

At the Wicklow Mountains, I felt peace,

Delightfully restraining the urge to run along a stream,

And with deep breaths, breathing in, just breathe,

There was a distinct sense of magic in the trees.

Oh, Ireland, you are my hearts home,

From shore to shore, I could roam,

From O'Conners Pub in Salt Hill reciting a poem,

To a pub nearby Dublin with a friend in tow.

All the wondrous nature you provide,

From the mossy trees to the seaside,

On a trip over to Aran Island,

That showed much of the old ways of Ireland.

I don't believe I will ever forget you,

In fact, my soul longs to visit anew,

This place that speaks to my soul with majestic views,

With fairy portals beaconing for you to step through.

COZUMEL

Oh, Cozumel, it was simply not our time,

I could appreciate your beauty only so much,

A less-than-compatible companion,

Lead me to armor myself up,

Still, I could appreciate your beauty,

And marvel at the color of the seas,

Our snorkeling was a little choppy,

And I couldn't see your wondrous reef.

The ruins were majestic, filled with history,

And on the wind, I could hear them whisper to me,

But ruins are a soft spot for me, absolutely,

And much preferable to the market, which was too salesy.

I wish I could have seen more in my time there,

But perhaps I will visit again with someone else to share,

The beautiful sights and sounds, the smell of the sea on the air,

And even more ruins to explore, even more to share.

GRIEF AND THE SEA

I would never have booked this trip if only I knew,

That one of my children had secretly withdrew,

He withdrew inside himself, and we didn't recognize the clues,

His mind was telling him some pretty harsh untruths.

He took his life a few months before this trip,

My partner at the time pointed to the non-refundable tickets,

It was obvious I would have to go through with this,

They said maybe it would help me step forward into happiness.

So, we traveled the sea on a large cruise ship,

I'm not even sure where it is that we really went,

But I do remember the sea, and how it penetrated my grief,

standing and seeing nothing but the ocean offered temporary relief.

I remember the highlight of the trip, where my grief lightened,

With the most amazing hug from a sweet sea lion,

And being able to pet and swim with a dolphin,

That seemed to be able to sense the state I was in.

I felt more understood in that very brief time,

By this empathic dolphin and sea lion,

Then, by the others that were still in my life,

Telling me to move on, telling me I shouldn't still cry.

NATURES PAINTER

I love to see the sun's rays dancing through the trees.

I look forward to the ever-changing colors of the leaves.

The color palette nature offers us is vibrant and vast,

As a painter, there is nothing more of her I could ask.

The moon and celestial sky offer so much vibrant light,

And the void around that light offers contrasts delight.

The shadows of the trees against a moonlit landscape,

They are as delightful as a sea cove or a mountain cave.

Nothing brings me as much joy and peace as nature herself,

From the gently lapping waves to the portals to other realms.

With every brush stroke, I struggle to capture her essence,

I know it pales in comparison to her first-hand presence.

THE OCEAN

The ocean, the source of many a poem.

Full of mysteries, and full of raging storms.

Far enough out it's humbling as you see nothing else for miles.

The ocean can offer serenity, when it's not being wild,

Ever in flux the ocean is, itself, unique.

An ever changing tide, curious brine, and legends of cities underneath.

On a day before a storm I loved to stop and play.

The ocean always rewarded me with the biggest of waves.

I love to dive deep into the comforting sea,

Unaware, that any moment a riptide could take me.

Oh, ocean, you are so cleverly deceptive.

You had me pulled beneath, and then out, should I feel rejected?

Why did you release me in time to save my life?

Did you know my future would hold so much strive?

I struggled to the surface searching desperately for the coast,

Frantically swimming in the swirling waves and crashing foam.

Did you help push me back towards the shore?

Twas this a foreboding premonition of the life had in store?

Oh, my ocean, if only I'd have listened, heeded your warning,

As you tried to teach me about life and growing.

But then again you still offer me perspective, when I see the ocean vast.

I am a speck on your surface, humbled, we're meant not to last.

CLOUDS

Remember when we used to search for shapes,

Each cloud our own ink blot test to take.

I think we always saw a unicorn of some kind,

And a dragon surrounded by unique design.

No cardboard or electronics were needed for this game,

And some of my fondest memories were giving the clouds names.

I remember when I used to think clouds would feel like blankets,

And I could sit on a big puff surrounded by it's mist.

My favorites used to be the cumulonimbus,

It's billowing fluffy structure reaching towards the heavens.

I'd imagine being in a huge swarm of clouds,

With magical shapes and cloud creatures all around.

I never gave much through, or concern to the thunderstorms,

They were just as beautiful as the fluffy clouds we so just before.

SPRING

It's coming, can you feel it?

The air itself has shifted,

Carrying on the wind a promise,

That is echoed in actions of the forest.

Whispering to us that the darkness must fade,

And fresh new beginnings are on their way.

As the breeze grows constantly warmer,

And the sunlight begins to stay a bit longer.

The trees and flowers in the forest are budding,

There can be no denying that spring is coming.

I'll be out planting perennials in the garden,

Fulfilling desires and needs that were starving.

It's seedtime now as we prepare,

To reap the benefits for our hard work and care.

Soon the buds will be beautifully flowering,

As they overcome the darkness by simply growing.

A STORM

I love a good storm raging all about,

With the winds whipping my hair and rain pouring down,

With each squall I feel a sense of being freed,

And the roaring of the thunder puts me at ease.

While others shy away from the blustering wrath,

I find comfort watching the lightning blast after blast.

As the tempestuous wind continues to wail,

I take further comfort in each and every gale.

Perhaps it mirrors the storms in my soul,

Or maybe the storm provides me a way to let go.

Another possibility is it offers me a promise,

There is beauty in and after all it's violence.

While I reveal in the storm, I see that no two are the same,

It reminds me, no matter how dark it gets, light returns to the day.

A SUNNY DAY

Nothing compares to a radiant sunny day,

Where you can bask in the sun as the clouds give way,

And splash in the pond or walk with nature,

And feel the luminous sun shimmer with splendor.

Nothing compares to the feeling of brilliant light,

Pouring over your skin, everything feels just right.

The clarion calls of birds ring pleasantly in your ears,

And the shinning wonderful sun continues to provide cheer.

For now the haze in your mind is burned away,

As you can't help but feel joy on this sunny day.

LESSONS FROM THE STORM

When the skies darken, creating night during the day,

I know it promises a light show and the musical sounds of thunder and rain.

Where others might see it as an inconvenience or bad omen,

I see it as nourishment for the earth and I relish in those moments.

Sometimes, I feel as though nature herself just needs an outlet,

The crashing sound of thunder and the crackling light are part of that,

Her way of screaming, her way of communicating her rage and her frustration,

Or perhaps her way of feeling deep sorrow, sobbing, as she feels devastation.

Like everything else in nature no two are the same,

I hear different songs in each and every single rain,

The thunder can be received differently as well, ominous at times,

And at others a sign of all that the water can provide.

One lesson remains the same with every thunderous break,

The storm will indeed pass and the light will return the sun fully awake,

No storm lasts forever, that is always the truth of the storm,

As the sky changed from light to dark, and it once again transforms.

Opening up to the sun, perhaps a rainbow will slide across the sky,

Offering, to everyone who is looking for it, a beautiful and magical sight,

The rainbow present after some of the worst storms is a symbol,

From the black and white landscape, the gift of color, it's simple.

The clouds obscured the sun temporarily to allow you to see,

That when the storm passes the rainbow is possible for you and me,

So when the storms of your life blow through and it seems dark,

Remember that you have only to wait out that particular storm.

· · ·

Once the storm has passed sharpen your attention to what is around,

Celebrate that you did not, as you feared, drowned,

See if you can find what was illuminated as the darkness lifts from your mind,

Perhaps you will find new colors to marvel at, new insights to find.

As the thunder rumbles through the sky while I sit here and type away,

I myself, find self reflection cathartic as my body vibrates wide awake,

The electricity from the lightning seeming to infiltrate my body without a touch,

I can see now, where I am is miles away from where I was.

Many storms have rolled through, be them storms of grief or storms of life,

Some even had me question if they were storms I could survive,

But here I sit, survive I did, and I can see things in the afterglow,

That at the time I refused to see or come to know.

The storm comes closer louder before receding to a gentle hum,

Simulating the waves of our many emotions,

The rain from torrential to gently soothing patters on the window,

My energy flows from wide open lulled slowly into ready for a light doze.

THE MOON

Tightly tied to my bodies tide,

The phases indicate when hormones rise.

The full moon brings the potential for life,

As the new moon brings me peace of mind.

The crescent offers me a silver smile,

And all the phases in between stir something wild.

Always I feel peace bathing in her light,

As she slides in an arc illuminating the night.

A powerful message she gives to us then,

Her and the stars brightening the darkness.

THE SUN

As I tilt my face to the sun in the summer,

I feel the freckles begin to dapple.

The warmth touches the depths of myself,

to the weariest parts, whispering of help.

My prescription for the winter blues,

flushing with vitamin D as I'm infused.

A natural uplifting alternative medicine,

that has no real pharmaceutical comparison.

It's rays reaching deep into the earth,

touching each seed and root, promising rebirth.

It's warmth considered a blessing and curse,

As it can give vital life, or it can brutally burn.

The balance is there if you cared to look,

for all we perceive as bad the Sun is good,

we can't live without it, that much we know,

I think it is critical to even humans growth.

As I close my eyes on a winter day,

hoping to feel at least a few of the suns rays,

to stave off the cold whipping wind from my face,

If I catch it just right the cold is momentarily replaced.

In the spring I delight in the spouts it summons,

watching everything come alive with promises of summer.

The lesson here is we are all capable of rebirth,

We can all survive the long winters were endure.

The summer brings with it playfulness and fun,

This is the center stage moment for the sun.

Thriving at it's peek it kiss us all on the cheek,

as it gives us everything it has for a few more weeks.

When the fall comes the sun is winding down,

the leaves start falling and turning shades of brown.

Though the sun still shines it has less time,

but this is all by a wonderful perfect design.

The sun ebbs and flows just as we all do,

another natural symbol that whispers, renew.

Another sign to reassure us that we are resilient,

That just like the sun we are all a little brilliant.

THE MAIDEN IN NATURE

Under the falling leaves, I would twirl,

But that was when I was a young girl,

I would run and jump into the big piles of leaves raked up,

All of nature has always been one of my greatest loves.

I would converse many a night under the sky,

Staring at the stars as if they were sparkling eyes,

Esoteric conversations, deep and meaningful, were born,

And I felt conviction of self, I felt absolutely sure.

I felt at home looking back out into the sky,

Or when I went traveling through the trees on a hike.

I felt calm, my mind stopped spinning out,

I know that it was because I was grounding now.

I would dance and spin under the moon,

Blissful and without fear of what others do.

It didn't matter if they would think I was strange

I felt connected in the strongest of ways.

I felt here, under the stars, I could be myself,

I could shine as I danced and twirled about,

Like a flame that knows it's only free for a time,

I felt completely free, with no reason to hide.

The ocean offered me the same kind of peace,

And perspective as I respected the vastness of the sea.

The birds sang a song that felt was just for me,

And the sand between my toes cooled my feet.

The smell of the salty air always brought me joy,

And remembering the castles we built for waves to destroy,

Nostalgic, I remember friends who have long forgotten me,

But always, I will always, have the sea and the trees.

I'm not sure there is a part of nature I don't marvel at,

Although some find it odd, I even like rats.

My whole life, I viewed furry critters as my friends,

I always felt seen by them through a different lens.

I've always felt just a little set apart in the human world,

I guess in nature I felt more like a safe little girl,

Safe to be myself, wild and free and all that entails,

Free to be all of me without being curtailed.

THE MOTHER IN NATURE

I was afraid for a while that nature would lose its awe,

As I went to college and began to learn what things are,

As if giving something a label took away its magic,

But what happened to me was the exact opposite.

As I grew from a maiden into a mother,

My appreciation deepened as I saw nature,

I appreciated all the ways it leant me a helping hand,

Sometimes by simply allowing me to walk on her land.

But a walk was so much more than it seemed,

As I began to grow my own gardens and I began to weed,

I started to understand even more about life as a whole,

See, a weed isn't bad; someone just decides it doesn't belong.

With every hole I dug and every plant placed,

I felt the earth give me my very own embrace,

Although my mother had passed, I had another,

The earth herself, after all, was all of our mother.

I, growing from a maiden into the role of a mother myself,

Could appreciate the duality of the role that I held,

I had become wiser than when I thought I knew it all,

And nature bore witness as she hurried me along.

Road trips through winding roads between mountains,

Gave me insight that I felt I was lacking,

Sometimes, I'd sit at the top of an overlook,

Life was suddenly less overwhelming from this view.

Perspective, the greatest gift a mother can give,

As every mother I know struggles to be their best,

Mother Earth reminds us that we are perfect just as we are,

It's a human concept to assign each other flaws.

How often I've seen a gnarled tree and found peace,

Knowing that even if I have flaws, I'm perfectly me,

Created with the ebb and flow of the world around us,

Embracing who we are, and who we can grow into is a must.

Nature showed me the growth mindset from the earliest of years,

Teaching resilience as trees seemed to die & leaves disappeared.

Only to burst forth with a brilliance in the spring,

If it could do that, perhaps I could do anything.

Seeds grow in total darkness compacted in dirt or sand,

But they don't give up; they emerge, and petals expand,

Caterpillars cocoon in a soft dark wrap,

Unaware, they will emerge with wings that flap.

Nature is full of examples: whispering, never give up,

Because just on the other side of the darkness is the sun.

It shows us time and again that no matter how small we may be,

We matter in ways we can't possibly see.

THE CRONE IN NATURE

Many people find the beauty in a running stream,

Or in a tree that is filled with blossoming leaves.

But what about when the stream is all dried up,

And the leaves on all the trees have gone?

I see the beauty in both a tree in full blossom or with naked branches,

And in the winter, I see a landscape filled with meaningful symbolism.

Even a decaying tree lying on the forest floor covered in moss,

Provides rich value to the forest as it becomes re-absorbed.

Nature herself offers us the greatest example of how we are one,

She shows us how we are all connected to a distant sun.

How we are all affected by even the subtle shifts in the ecosystem,

And how we all matter more than we've grown accustomed.

Even parts of nature that seem barren or harsh to our human eyes,

Play a magical and important part in species able to thrive.

What a lesson for us to learn when we have difficult people in our lives,

When we feel like some people caused us to barely survive.

There are so many lessons in nature, of resilience and adaptation,

That they deserve our full and committed consideration,

As we struggle and we feel we might not survive another transformation,

Let nature reassure us; let her provide us with the proper motivation.

We are capable of turning to someone older than any of our time,

When we turn to Mother Earth for the most powerful of advice.

We realize that everything created by her is perfect by design,

And no matter our faith we can find in her a special guide.

Take comfort, that we have seen the harshest conditions transformative.

We have seen things that seemed dead come alive and become restorative.

All of that happens around us every single day, simply by design.

So, in your hardest moments, remember you're just getting ready to thrive.

Your Nature Free-Writing

YOUR NATURE FREE-WRITING

I invite you to join me in a free writing session.

Have you ever taken a walk in nature and felt better? Have you experienced joy after working in a garden? Have you searched your TV apps for nature landscapes and watched them? Take a few moments to write about a memory or observation you have with nature. If you can take a walk, practice being aware and present with the natural world around you. If you can't, find some nature shows or YouTube for a relaxing nature video. What do you feel? What comes to mind? Allow it to flow through you to these pages.

Your Nature Poem(s)

YOUR NATURE POEM(S)

I invite you to read your free writing and look for any poetry in it. Sometimes circling words that rhyme can help you see patterns. Use it as inspiration to write your own nature poems, or just let the poetry flow through you.

Other Realms

Spirit connection,
Journeying through realms,
I have found my home.

When I lost my mom at fifteen, I had a severe faith crisis. How could all these terrible things happen if everything I had been taught were true? I started to read everything I could on many different faiths to make sense of the Catholicism I was raised with. I studied many, including Buddhism, Toltec Wisdom, Shamanism, and various forms of paganism. The older faiths seemed to resonate with me more. I have always had a soft spot for older lore. My deep love for many cultures and different spiritualities and my contemplations of them spilled into my poetry. This chapter is not religious in any way that would require you to abandon your faith to read it. I did several years of apprenticeship in Shamanism at a wonderful place in Vermont called Spirit Hollow, and I loved that they embraced people of all faiths. They never once asked anyone to put their faith aside or below the teachings they offered. I have always loved that about many of the more ancient faiths. So, please take what resonates and leave the rest. This is a place of otherworldly nuggets.

TIME

Through time, the watches fall,

Through the air, the sun shines,

And everything comes back to time.

The trees call out to me,

The air whispers softly.

Brilliance is a state of mind,

The trees are made brilliant through time,

Everything seems like a lie,

The only true thing is time.

A circle of life is a circle of time,

Everything seems in a bind,

The clocks are ticking in your mind,

And it's all about time.

MY LIGHT

Deafening silence fills my ears,

I have hurt through all these years.

Love has been lost and not yet found,

And in my self-pity, I could have drowned.

I emerge from the swirling waters of life,

A new being composed of light.

I will continue on and not be defeated,

As I have learned of life's many secrets.

If you dare to defy the universal laws,

Then you shall never learn them at all.

Think instead upon what you see,

A circle of life or a circle of eternity.

Respect the love even as it is lost,

And you will find life's not that hard.

Look to the Universe and nature around you,

And you may learn, so as not to be fooled.

Faith comes in many names,

None of which involves fortune and fame.

Learn to understand the concept of peace,

Only then will you come to walk with me.

FATHER TIME

Father time,

Take me home,

Don't leave me here all alone.

Father time,

I am your child,

I believe in my heart I won't be exiled.

Father time,

I love you so,

You are the power the world loves.

Father time,

Please don't forget me,

I know that you won't because you love me.

Father time,

Please help me,

To turn my dreams into reality.

Father time

I am your child,

Love me forever. I am your child.

Father time,

Teach me everything,

Give me knowledge as well as wisdom.

Father time,

Take me home,

Take me to that place filled with love.

AN ANGEL

An Angel,

Is she dressed in white?

Does she take to flight?

An Angel,

Is she here or there?

Is she everywhere?

An Angel

Can be a person,

Someone you know well.

An Angel

Can be an actress,

So, you really can't tell.

An Angel

Has an inner beauty,

Most people can see.

An Angel

Her voice is like the wind,

Her eyes are like the sea.

An Angel

Is so much more sweet,

Then anything we eat.

An Angel

In your life may be,

Someone you can't see.

An Angel

Has an innocence,

That no one around can see.

An Angel

Has a purity,

That is meant to be.

An Angel,

Is such beauty and such love,

Who should know an angel? All of us.

DRAGON RIDERS

The wind through your hair,

The smell of burnt air,

And the warmth of the fire,

Makes you a dragon rider.

Nor wind nor rain, snow nor sleet,

Could ever compare to a dragon fleet.

If I could, I would fly higher than the sky,

And it would be the universe I would pass by.

With a dagger by your side,

I will fight for what is mine,

As day by day goes by,

You carefully fly high.

INVISIBLE FRIEND

I saw a boy who wasn't there,

He smiled at me and said,

"How do you dare?"

I turned around to answer,

Or ask I might say,

And he disappeared just as fast as he came!

The very next day, I saw him again,

He looked at me and said,

"I am your friend."

"If you are my friend,

"Then why did you leave me?"

I asked the boy naturally.

No one can be there every minute,

And all the time,

The best that I can do is just to try.

The boy disappeared again,

But this time I knew,

It wouldn't be long; he wasn't quite through.

A PICTURE PERFECT WOMAN

A picture-perfect woman,

Sat in a picture-perfect chair,

Rocking back and forth,

As if she hadn't a care.

She was as beautiful as can be,

With long black hair,

And sometimes it felt to me,

As if she wasn't really there.

She was peaceful and calm,

But her temper could flair,

She helped me out a lot,

The woman was always fair.

I believe that her beauty,

Came from somewhere deep within,

She would help if she could,

And she would never give in.

I feel as if I know her,

She comes to visit now and then,

I look forward to every day,

To feel her presence again.

VISIT

"Sweet child," I heard her say,

"I have come to visit you today."

"Do not be frightened by my appearance."

"I may still talk despite my transparence."

"I have come to bid you hello."

"My girl, I did not wish to scare you so."

"I will leave you, if you only wish,"

"But I am here to give a list."

"A list but of three things for you,"

"None of them have to do with school,"

"Number one says take it slow,"

"I do wish you wouldn't rush about so."

"And for the second, my little dove,"

"Don't try so hard to please your love,"

"He will love you more and more every day,"

"And you needn't worry where he'll stay."

"Finally, the third comes to mind."

"With this last thought, the woman sighed."

"Clear your mind of negative thoughts."

"That's when you'll find the richest pot!"

"Like the pot of gold at the end of the rainbow,"

"Your inner beauty will start to grow."

"I turned around, and I saw nothing."

"But I knew the woman was simply hiding."

She was hiding and waiting until the next time,

The next time, I could go away and fly.

THE SOUNDS

Sweet sorrow, said the girl,

The girl whose life had,

Crumbled down and lever her all alone,

To stand only on her own.

Sweet sadness, said the woman,

The woman who had no one,

No one to run to or talk to,

So that she barely made it through.

Sweet sorrow, said the girl.

Who spoke ancient fairy lore,

That she heard easing through the door,

Still, 'twas far away, and she was alone.

Sweet sadness, said the woman,

The woman whose life was inside out,

And upside down until she heard,

The odd sounds, very beautiful odd sounds.

Sweet forgiveness sighed the girl,

The girl who was drawn into the fairy world.

The fairy world with a sound so sweet,

The sorrowful girl began to weep.

Sweet joy, said the woman,

The woman drawn to the sounds,

Of a harp and a pipe and was no longer alone,

Sweet sounds she whispered 'twas a boon.

Sweet forgiveness, said the girl,

The girl who danced to her precious lore,

The very same lore heard outside her door,

That she so very much adored.

Sweet joy, said the woman,

The woman who was all alone,

With no one around to turn to,

No one left to hold her left with no one.

Sweet sadness, said the woman,

The woman who was quiet and still,

As the last of her memory,

Danced away the last of her will.

MY CASTLE

On top of a hill,

In the thick, deep woods,

Sits a castle, I see,

The one castle I love.

Next to the trees,

I stand, and I watch,

I watch for the castle,

The mean castle guards.

They come running through,

With their sword in hand,

They don't let anyone enter,

They protect this land.

Where I am is not,

Their concern right now.

I step into the shadows,

And they miss me somehow.

I know all the tricks,

In the books I have read.

They couldn't catch me,

If I were painted red.

Now they are past me,

Running still more.

While they ignore me,

I'm beginning to soar.

Through the woods,

On legs like a leopard,

They'll never see me,

Through trees that are herds.

The trees pull together,

Masking my movement,

The trees keep me safe,

If only for a moment.

Finally, I reached it,

The beautiful castle.

I look up in awe,

And I reach for my lasso.

Suddenly, I falter,

I'm beginning to fall,

"Time to come home, Lady,"

I hear them call.

Into the castle,

I go without warning,

To get ready for dinner,

And a great housewarming.

BY THE OCEAN

Sitting by the ocean,

Watching the Green Sea.

As the waves crash down,

They reach out and touch my feet.

Suddenly, they retreat,

Erasing all of the tracks,

That lovers had been making,

Imprints of their feet or their backs,

They see me once again,

And they come crashing up to me once more,

As if to let me know somehow,

That it is me that they adore.

Slowly, I get up,

And walk to the line of foam,

Watching as I start to walk,

The crashing waves were so bold.

The now disappearing sea,

Withdraws its cool touch,

But as it leaves me again,

It gifts me with good luck.

I soon begin to fade,

And as I slowly disappear,

I will wait again in silence,

For this time next year.

REVENGE FOR HER DEATH

Her grave is silent now,

And her soul is growing loud.

She has come back because of someone,

Who has tried to put her down?

He came into her family,

And then tore them apart,

And I'm sorry to say,

She died with a broken heart.

She waited until dark,

Before making her appearance.

Then she found her family,

Though still, that is mysterious.

She wanders around,

Circling my bed at night,

And when the sun comes up,

She takes flight.

She came to me over,

And over again.

Until I realized,

She wanted revenge.

MY FRIEND

Sometimes I feel you watching me,

In the tough times, I miss you terribly.

In the toughest, I can almost feel your touch,

And sometimes it's just not enough.

I need you here to hold me when I cry.

A hug always helped dry my eyes.

Your advice was always kind and true.

There is no one here that could replace you.

MUSIC SAVED ME

Everyone has the blues.

It only matters what you will do.

I gave my heart away to the music.

Swirly and dancing in my mind.

I watch a soul twisting to the music.

Writing and dancing along with mine.

SPARE SOUL ROOM

There's a room people go to, and I don't know quite why.

It's called the spare soul room, where everyone hears cries.

Sometimes, I wonder if that's where I'll end up.

In the spare soul room where no one is so tough.

No one has control of all the pain that they will feel.

The spare soul room itself will not let you heal.

Your only goal now is not to go there.

To the spare soul room just to get a spare.

Now that you know, I'm sure that you're glad.

That you've always kept the soul you've always had.

IN LOVE WITH A GHOST

He never wishes to see me falling apart.

I know that he will protect me from any harm,

I feel loved and safe in his arms,

And I can trust him enough to give my whole heart.

I am in love with a man that is not there,

Yet, in this life, there is so much we share.

Our passions and love reach across time,

Our souls are destined to one day entwine.

DANCING WITH SPIRIT

I've been alone, but not alone, longer than I should,

I feel a spirit next to me as I dance under the moon,

Slipping to my back I feel him breathing on my neck,

His hands caress my sides, and for him, I continue to dance.

His hands, the way they touch me, it's pure magic,

His fingers across my lips are just the way I want it,

Fingertips across my cheek, and I feel passion welling,

This seduction is a two-way street; our touch is too compelling.

I've kept my passion hidden safely away from all,

All but the spirit that dances with me against the odds.

I've not felt that touch across my skin, except from him,

For years, I kept my passion and all my desires in check.

I lay my head down on his chest, but he is not there,

My passion begs to be released, but who's earned its share,

He is a spirit who dances with me on lonely nights,

I can almost feel him touch me, and it feels so right.

He would want me to be happy, to find another love,

But without him, I am not sure I can; I feel so very lost.

I miss the dance I danced when my spirit was pure,

Before all the horror, all the lies, deceit, and hurt.

I dance once more, sister machine gun, burn,

He wraps his arms around me once more,

I'm so safe in his arms, safer than any other ghost,

I revel in the passion I feel before I realize I am still alone.

LOVE THROUGH THE VEIL

Away, I fall into the darkness.

My heart is filled with sorrow.

I wait to be rescued by my prince,

Hoping a brighter day comes tomorrow.

I fell further into the black pit.

Away from all light and love.

I lost all my hope and never knew it,

And today, I search again for love.

I grasp love and hold it close and dear,

And I find my eyes searching yours.

I feel you hold me tightly near,

As the hours pass through open doors.

But you are not really here.

SAMHAIN

I am one with the universe.

With love, I connect to thee,

I ask that the past be laid to rest,

And once more for the removal of negativity.

May thy slate once again shine,

With hope, confidence, and love,

May our stories blossom in the coming year,

And our dreams are realized and won.

May we never forget our ancestors,

May they be with us through it all,

And on this night of Samhain,

May they come near and hear our call.

With our lives intertwined,

With friends and family by our side,

May we move from this year to the next,

Taking only the most positive of steps.

FAE HERITAGE

In my heritage, they leave out honey and milk for the Fae,

Beautiful little tricksters that love to come in and play,

And when things go missing around the house,

You can politely ask them to help you browse.

Stories of the Fae range from evil tricksters to helpful beauties,

I think it all depends on you, and what you want to see.

It is quite possible, even the habit of many to knock on wood,

Draws the Fae in to bring the person knocking good luck.

It was said the tradition came from knocking on trees,

To bring forward gods, or spirits to avoid bad luck with ease,

But the origins of the Fae are much bigger than they seem,

The former Celtic gods used their powers to become Sidhe.

So, you see, I would never call them wicked, descendants of gods,

Of the Tuatha De Danann, I have always been quite fond,

I love their stories and the light that they bring forth,

And I see the Fae as just another extension of that form.

So, I'll keep leaving out honey and milk on special days,

And I am not really bothered by those that don't get my ways.

I'll keep knocking on wood, hoping it brings a little good,

And hoping my gifts and little ways are, by them, understood.

DRAGON SLEEP

When I was a young girl, I loved mythical creatures,

Dragons and unicorns, I was one of those believers.

Someone gave me a poster as a child with myths of both,

I'd be torn about what side I would bring forth.

The dragon still scared me just a little bit,

Society had definitely made a big deal about it,

Unicorns were more acceptable, it would seem,

With their majestic innocence and purity.

As I got older, I had nightmares about things a child shouldn't know,

My mom told me one day, to think of unicorns and they would come.

So, the next nightmare while in the dream, I thought of one,

And she came to me, protected me, and away we would run.

Over time, as we grow, we forget quite a lot,

I'd have nightmares, and no one would save me, I forgot.

I forgot I could just call or picture them in my mind,

I suffered through these nightmares for quite some time.

Years went by, and I accumulated even more tragedy,

It seemed unrealistic for so much to happen to a teen,

But I found a few books that helped me in between,

And I rediscovered this technique in my early twenties.

I was reading a book on dragons, and it said to sit and meditate,

I diligently closed my eyes, trying to get my mind to stay,

I wanted a fierce protector to help me finally feel safe,

A beautiful mother dragon came to me on that day.

I made a new practice each night before I would sleep,

I would imagine being nestled comfortably under her wing,

Her shining, gleaming scales of metallic green,

With her mothering eye watching gently over me.

Finally, I could sleep as dragons and unicorns watched over me,

I no longer had to fear the nightmares; I could bring them into my dreams.

And if a nightmare began, they would come and change the scene,

I know it is strange to some, but I'm grateful for the peaceful dragon sleep.

BRIGID

A day, a day all dedicated to you,

So powerful you were, you couldn't be subdued,

Bridging the oldest and most ancient beliefs,

When you became adopted into the new.

A patroness of healing and the eternal flame,

You can be called on to heal the pain,

A symbol of fertility and light,

You can be called on to make things right,

A muse to any who would sit to write,

Particularly fond of poets with the sight,

And any who turn their hand to smithing,

Can hear her on the wind, gently whispering.

Her spirit transcended multiple planes,

And some say she continues to this day,

So if you need justice or inspiration,

Brigid, speak it, say her name.

THE OTHERWORLDLY MAIDEN

Growing up, I didn't quite know what the world was made up of,

It seemed it was just a traumatic event after another while I sought love.

I sought love from all the wrong places, and I didn't know quite why,

I had suffered abuse and loss, but I had faith until my mom died.

I was bereft, floating in some weird suspended time and space,

Everyone else's life seemed to bustle on right in front of my face.

I felt separate, lost, somehow completely displaced.

I was trapped in some weird reality that I couldn't escape.

A friend gave me a book one day when she found me in tears,

It set me off on a path of voraciously reading about faiths for years.

I read about Buddhism, Toltec wisdom, Shamanism, Tao, and many more,

I simply could not go back to the person I was before.

Quite a few years later, when suicide touched our lives,

I would find myself reading *the Four Agreements* as I cried.

This wisdom was valuable, and *The Secret* was also combined.

But, I found myself concerned child victims would be left behind.

See, the universal law of attraction that they teach focuses on thought,

They say everything that has happened to you is your fault.

This was a hard thing for me to accept, knowing about child assaults,

Surely, the universe wouldn't deliver these horrors to someone so small.

But I wasn't supposed to think this way; that is me sabotaging myself,

I should just accept what happened was good for the higher self,

This didn't make sense; it didn't quite fit, but I was in love with the rest,

This seemed like something I just had to learn about and address.

Alas, I wasn't that brave as a maiden, I wouldn't speak out to the world,

Telling them that they are alienating these little boys and girls,

And arguably, they need to learn this law of attracting the most,

But an epiphany would come much later, after the mother, as crone.

THE OTHERWORLDLY MOTHER

My mother had left this plane; she was on the other side,

I swore I'd never be a mother, but that was not for me to decide,

I took in two kids, and that was when I wanted to turn to her for advice,

Blessed, the universe had given me other mothers in which to confide.

Nothing teaches you quite like parenting others can,

Seeing the challenges you must have presented firsthand,

I never wanted to call my mother and apologize so badly,

If I had a time machine I would have done it differently gladly.

I was grateful I started my journey to better connect to the universe,

Prior to having kids, it set me up to be of better service.

If I hadn't found the many techniques offered through faith,

I think I would have struggled more when they inevitably misbehaved.

I was able to teach my kids different meditation techniques,

And tried to teach them how to grow and find inner peace,

All the while, I was teaching myself as well, to breathe,

Whenever they came home and told me of another kid's critiques.

I learned that no one is perfect, and we all fall down sometimes,

But those teachable moments are invaluable moments to shine,

And accidents can sometimes be a happy surprise,

But no matter how much you give, there is only so much you can provide.

You can't make them listen or adopt your way of life,

And you have to accept that one day, they will say goodbye,

Leaving for their own life, that you trained them to survive,

You have to let go, the hardest part, and hope they will thrive.

I wonder if this is what our ancestors go through when we struggle,

I wonder if they are as torn, watching us get into trouble.

Taking a step outside of ourselves, and watching from a distance,

How hard must this be for anyone or anything omniscient?

Is it possible, regardless of your deity, they just want us to be free,

Is it really as simple, as letting go, to gain everything you dreamed?

Can we really stop the rat race and peacefully achieve,

Perhaps the otherworldly mother's greatest lesson is to be open to receive.

THE OTHERWORLDLY CRONE

Oh, my child, she would say to her younger self,

With no hint of condescension, seeking only to help,

And only when she was ready or came to her herself,

Knowing if she pushed too hard she might simply rebel.

She accepts that sometimes others are not ready,

To receive wisdom from someone Otherworldly.

No, she knows, exactly when and where to impart her wise words,

And if we are ready to receive, those words are heard.

We sense them, feel them in our hearts and in our souls,

They whisper to us, and sometimes, yell at us to let go.

One of the hardest things we will likely ever have to do,

When our tendency is to try and control, sometimes subdue.

Yet, the Otherworldly Crone is very clear on this point,

You have to let go, to manifest the life that you want.

Release everything you think you have to do, and listen to your heart,

Let it lead you, and know it will be okay when paths start to part.

The otherworldly crone wants only the best for those who are good,

She leaves you signs in numbers, and symbolism if you look.

If you commit to a growth mindset, she will help you grow,

But be warned, sometimes situations will get uncomfortable.

She sees us when we get comfortable when we get stagnant,

And when we start to accept things we shouldn't accept.

She knows we do this because it is familiar, and familiar is comfortable,

But comfortable won't get us to the places that we deserve to go.

So, she has to make us a little uneasy as she shakes things up a bit,

And we find ourselves with a bit more in the way of challenges.

You could look at it like a test, but I think it's more of a rite of passage,

Taking you forward and preparing a future you'll have the advantage.

One of the greatest lessons I learned when I became a crone,

Was that I had power, but I had even more power when I let go,

It was up to me to challenge the stories of my past created by trauma,

I re-wrote them entirely, now able to manifest; the block was gone.

Your Otherworldly Free-Writing:

YOUR OTHERWORLDLY FREE-WRITING:

I invite you to join me in a free writing session.

Have you ever had a crisis of faith? Have you ever felt so close to your source or god you felt tremendous peace? Have you found a belief system that just resonated with your soul? Even if you don't follow a faith, you can curiously observe those who do. I invite you to write about anything that moves you. What speaks to your soul?

Your Otherworldly Poem(s):

YOUR OTHERWORLDLY POEM(S):

Read your free writing and look for any poetry in it. Use it as inspiration to write your own otherworldly poems, or just let the poetry flow through you. Sometimes circling words that rhyme can help you see patterns.

Resilience and Inspiration

Find inspiration,
In your awesome resilience,
You are still standing.

I started this book knowing I wanted to end with a spectacular chapter all about positive messages and rising above. Alas, though the words and poems in this chapter are about resilience and inspiration they are not written cavalierly, or lightly. Sometimes they are slow to rise, or just beginning to rise, so at times it is a subtle but honest chapter that I hope still hits the mark for offering you inspiration and encouraging resilience. This chapter is not simply positive for the sake of positivity; it is the result of the deep, grueling work of healing. It is an honest representation of the possibilities, lessons and inspiration that life has given me as I journeyed through my wreckage to brighter days. I hope you read these words and invoke for yourself the blessings, the inspiration, the healing, the resilience, the inspiration, the tenacity, and anything else that might help you step forward boldly into a brighter future for yourself.

A BLESSING

Let your inner beauty shine.

Let your dreams be free.

Let your passion never die.

May your life be all it can be.

In the darkness of the night,

Feel at peace under the moon,

Let the stars offer a comfort,

And sense of belonging like no other.

SIDESTEP

In the silence of my thoughts,

I acknowledge the hurt and pain,

Sidestep bitterness and resentment,

And simply go my own way.

I WILL NOT GIVE IN

There is a darkness that haunts me,

It wants to steal my light,

It wants everything,

It wants me to be terrified,

But I won't give in,

No, I will continue towards what's right,

For courage isn't the absence of fear,
But choosing to move forward and fight.

I WILL FIGHT

They suck the life force out of you,

Yet tell you you're here to be better.

They laugh at you and take from you,

Until you can breathe no longer.

They will take all you can give,

And more than you can afford.

And tell you, you need to be here,

To go anywhere in the world.

You take my money and all my time,

And laugh at mistakes that are mine,

Thinking you're better off the whole time,

Waiting for me to crack and then cry.

To hell with you and your school,

I could learn on my own.

It was my choice to come here,

And I will stay even if I stay alone.

You will not bring me down,

I will rise above all that I can,

To show you what it's all about,

I will stay and fight and I will win.

UNBREAKABLE

Unbreakable, I will still Shine,

Though they tried to drain all my light,

I may have been shattered, but never defeated,

I'll heal the fractures, and negative you created,

I give it back, you carry the weight of it,

I don't want it anymore; you can see how it fits.

I can tell you, you're already dead,

You can't survive all the things that you did.

I'm stronger, I refused to let you win,

Now I give it back to you, all of it.

Can you feel it pulling you down,

That black hole you created in me is yours now.

I survived it, but you will not,

I give you back every feeling and every thought.

I give you all the pain you gave to me,

Everything I carried inside for years, you see,

I blamed myself for your atrocities,

But now I know you were just an evil seed,

Your justifications matter little if at all,

I was a child, you were not, here's a curveball,

You wanted my light, so greedily,

To make you feel taller or stronger it seems,

I take it all back, every part of me,

And give you back all your darkness to be buried.

LOST WITHIN MYSELF

When he left, he took a part of me, took the life and light right out of me.

I didn't realize then what was done to me.

I spiraled into darkness, denial, and fatigue,

Several years later I realized I was no longer me.

I do not know what his true intentions were for me,

It is possible he did not intend to take these things to keep,

I do know that I was shattered into many pieces,

Slowly I realized that I had to collect back all of me.

Another came to collect the damaged pieces,

I struggled against myself, unable to see them.

I was lost for years, my light extinguished.

Lost and broken just drifting silent anguish.

Curiously, I was not aware of my situation or state,

Until I was awoken by an intense desire to feel complete.

This flame flickered and quickly started to grow strong,

I knew, suddenly I knew something was horribly wrong.

Where did she go, the free dancing spirit within me?

The girl I was, was so creative, loving, romantic, and free.

I set out on a mission certain to lead to self-discovery,

My soul is crying out for release, I know I must always be me.

PERSEVERANCE

She fell and got right back up laughing as she dusted herself off,

She tried again without fear that the result would be the same,

If you were to point out the potential failure, she would just scoff.

Later she would follow her dreams, convinced she could achieve them,

But the people she trusted tore her down and she quickly faltered,

Over time she rose back up, unwilling to quit, to tackle her dreams again.

Then she lost someone to cancer, another to suicide, and another, she fell,

Into despair, grief, into the darkest unending night she had ever known,

Seeming like forever she crawled forward; this was not her place to dwell.

Moving through obstacles and unfortunate events in her life many times,

When she wanted to succumb to emotions and to give up,

Each time this happened she dug deeper and began the climb.

Perseverance was a trait she never gave much thought to all,

Until it saved her life, and gave her back her dreams and voice,

And most importantly, she survived and learned how to stand tall.

COMPLEX GIRL

Too sensitive, over-emotional, and naive they called her,

Never realizing these were all symptoms of the trauma she endured.

He saw through her, straight to the demons of her past,

He held her anyway, comforting, strong, gentle, and steadfast.

They questioned how she could see good, have faith, and stay positive,

She was coping, it had to happen for a reason, or it didn't make sense.

Sometimes she moved on from her past out of sheer spite and defiance,

No one gets to have power over me, they certainly don't deserve compliance.

A FLOWERS IMPACT

Small steps forward are all you need,

You do not instantly grow into a flower from a seed,

Instead, you struggle as a sprout in the darkness,

Covered in heavy soil, entirely surrounded.

When the right season comes, you sense the light,

And you wiggle your way up, continuing to rise,

One day you are completely unseen,

Next, you replace a barren landscape with a dot of green.

Then you struggle to grow even more,

And though you are delicate you weather the storms,

Your stem grows stronger and there is a little bud,

That isn't quite ready to bloom or be plucked.

The sun shines down giving much-needed nourishment,

And the bud begins to open up with leaves so delicate,

The birds rejoice and nature hums as bees make contact,

This one flower blooming didn't know it had a massive impact.

RISE

Rise from the depths of your grief,

Give yourself permission to feel relief.

Rise from the scars of your past,

Give yourself permission to laugh.

Rise from the abuse and the pain,

Give yourself permission to dance in the rain.

Rise from the trauma you're working to heal,

Give yourself permission to feel.

Rise from the relationships that were tough,

Give yourself permission to love.

Rise from the chaos as it gives you a shake,

Give yourself permission to feel stable and safe.

UNLIMITED

You are unlimited,

Powerful and energetic.

You are limitless.

Powerful and compassionate.

POSITIVELY POSSIBLE

If you think positive, positive things will come,

The words of my grandmother barely a hum,

Echoing in my mind beckoning me to try,

So I started an experiment, based on words of the wise.

But that wasn't all she said to me that day,

This was a much larger lesson she tried to convey.

Thoughts become, words, they become dreams it's true,

but action is also required for the dreams you pursue.

She told me stay positive and I diligently tried,

Looking for the lessons or applying the silver line.

For the most part it worked, my mind began to change,

No longer focusing on the negative exchanging,

I could see the benefits, the lessons, the good instead,

And my mood, my emotions, they were instantly lifted.

I hadn't realized how many negative thoughts I regularly had,

But this blessing she gave me had the power to retrain my head.

So I kept at it through all the years, vision boards and dreams,

Seeing what I wanted and almost all I have actually achieved.

I still faltered and there were some times I couldn't apply it,

In the deepest depths of my grief, the entire principle I'd denied.

Faltering in the moments I may have needed it the most,

I turned to self-help books and those that saw the ghosts,

Of my lost child, and sister, and mother and my advisor and friend.

I busied myself as much as I could but the pain would not end.

I came back to the lessons my grandmother had taught me,

We are all different, and we all see life differently,

Yet we know what we focus on is where our energy flows,

So why wouldn't I want my energy on things that help me grow?

Why wouldn't I prefer more of the positive than the negative?

THE RESILIENT MAIDEN

The maiden has always been a resilient soul,

She survived having, in her heart, a black hole,

It seemed it would suck everything into the darkness,

But the maiden always rebelled, she'd have none of it.

Even when she was uncertain, a part of her knew,

That she had the power to always make it through.

Her naivety, sometimes a weapon, could be an asset too,

And she could come out the other side feeling renewed.

Her rose-colored glasses, dangerous but effective,

Kept her seeing things from a positive perspective,

The Resilient Maiden can indeed survive anything,

She is the seed that blooms into a flower in the spring.

Sometimes surrounded by pressure and darkness.

But determined that she will see the sun, she'll make it.

She is stubborn and resourceful, so she finds solutions,

And she seeks her own continuous evolution.

Concerned with love and the beauty of the world,

She's also interested in how she can best serve,

Not allowing herself to become cold or hard,

Instead of being bitter at them, she loved her scars.

They were lessons that had be taught to her,

A reminder of what she had learned,

And she knew that every scar that healed,

If the lesson was learned it provided her with a shield.

THE RESILIENT MOTHER

You came from the depths of something you didn't think you could survive,

A loss from which any mother would struggle to believe they could ever thrive.

You did the very best that you could, with all the knowledge and tools you had,

There were many days that would leave you stressed out, frustrated, or sad.

You took the bullets, angry words pelted at you from mouths that you fed,

And you still offered to tuck them or read a story when it was time for bed.

You tried to be perfect, but acknowledged when you came up short,

You laughed and crawled with them through the pillow and blanket forts.

When the electric company shut down your power, you told a little lie,

It was a part that had gone bad, don't let them know you are struggling to get by.

You rallied and swallowed your pride and asked for help when things went too far,

And those lights were on the very next day, as you explained that you received the part.

You were grateful to those who helped you from the smallest to the largest tasks,

And perhaps you would have done things differently if you could travel back to the past.

But only if you could take all the knowledge, you have now with you as you traveled,

And only if you could keep trying until you could prevent the tragedy from unraveling.

You cried yourself to sleep many nights even as the children believed everything was fine,

And smiled the next day just hoping everyone would happily get by.

It wasn't just the day-to-day stress and the tragic loss of a child that you endured,

But all the trauma from your past that you tried steadfastly to heal from or ignore.

Then there were the relationships, that you never seemed to get quite right,

And the stress that came as you tried to balance your family life with the increasing fights.

And even before you were a mother there was so much you had to recover from,

From the abusive relations, abandonment, and, yes, even the assaults.

Yet, there you were, expecting yourself to never lose your cool, never feel that rage,

And when you did you'd turn it inside on yourself and it becomes this kind of shame.

Until that day when everything changed, and you experienced the most difficult thing to date,

Everything, from what used to matter, to what felt like stress, everything changed that day.

You learned the deepest and darkest grief, the worst trauma you could have seen,

And though it took you time, you moved forward purposely and diligently.

You sought the help you needed to continue to show up as best you could for your family,

Even as they threw doors in your face, raged, or tossed blame your way casually.

None of that matters anymore, you learned nothing would ever be the same,

You had to cultivate a new normal, you had to find, for your life, new ways.

The work was hard, it was long, and you felt like giving up on several occasions.

It would have been easier, you thought at times, to just slip away into oblivion.

But you pressed on, despite or in spite of the pain depending on the day,

And you began to work on deeper issues like the root of your blame and shame.

You worked on your self-love, boundaries, gratitude and self-reflection,

Determined to do better, be better, and live a life of purposeful introspection.

At times you cut the world out, it was easier, he said you made them uncomfortable,

With your grief hanging off you like a worn-out safety comforter.

So, you would handle it on your own, but that wasn't very different for you after all,

You've done that your whole life, handling things it seems, others never saw.

Even with all of that, you continued on this journey, the path towards healing more,

And you rose like the phoenix from the ashes of a past that offered you mostly scars.

Determined to set right all that was wrong, from the generational teaching you received,

To heal the damage that often came from a girl that was just a little too naive.

You worked, and toiled, and did everything you were assigned by the healers,

Pressing forward and taking notes that you might share with any others.

A whisper in your mind saying, why, if I can't at least share what I have learned.

Why, if I can't at least try to prevent someone else from feeling this hurt.

This isn't a tale of a spontaneous resilient rise from petty grievances,

No, this is an authentic tail of what it looks like to cultivate true resilience.

It's ugly and it's hard, and it doesn't come from a perfect life with no hardships,

It comes from failures and falls, injuries and scars, as you learn to get up after being hit.

Every mother experiences this, and yet we all struggle to let our children fall,

Trying to protect them, to at least reduce the potential scars.

Sometimes it seems our very efforts produce the opposite of our intent,

Perhaps they rebel, perhaps they're headstrong, or we are rejected.

That doesn't stop us from trying to share our wisdom or mother others,

We learned the lessons so of course this advice, these lessons we offer.

The truth behind our resilience is that we knew we had choices to make,

And sometimes all the choices seemed awful, but we made them anyway.

Other times we had to make the choice we didn't think we could, or didn't want to,

But we did, either for our loved ones or because it was the only way through.

Sometimes it pissed us off, that we had to make a choice at all,

But we chose a path towards happiness even when we wanted to wallow.

It's the series of choices we make even when we feel defeated,

That keeps us moving forward, that makes it possible to dream again.

It's knowing that sometimes things will quite simply just suck,

But we can and will get through it, for us or the ones we love.

It's knowing that you don't have to be prepared for every scenario,

Because you have the one thing you will always need if you are resourceful.

It's raging against that good advice but knowing you'll follow it anyway,

Because you've learned that your emotions are largely temporary.

You know now that it's true, happiness is indeed a choice,

You might not always feel like it is, but cultivate your inner voice.

And not the one of the critic that is all doom and gloom, blame and shame,

No, cultivate the inner child, the intuition, it wants to keep you safe.

You are more resilient than you will ever truly know,

And you can always cultivate your resilience and help it grow.

THE RESILIENT CRONE

Of all that life has had to throw your way,

You have struggled, yes, but all, you overcame.

There is no greater testament to your strength,

Then the fact that you are still with us here today.

Your Resilience Free-Writing:

YOUR RESILIENCE FREE-WRITING:

I invite you to join me in a free writing session.

Where could you be more resilient, where can you see that you are. Write about anything that moves you. What speaks to your soul?

Your Resilience Poem(s)

YOUR RESILIENCE POEM(S)

I invite you to read through your free writing and look for any poetry in it.
Use it as inspiration to write your own *resilient* poems or just let the poetry
flow through you. Sometimes circling words that rhyme can help you see
patterns.

Ashes of the Phoenix

Someone looked at me once upon seeing a dark phoenix in a movie,

He said, "that is you, with all your trauma and history let loose on the city."

I felt it then her rage, her pain, the outrage, they were all mine,

I had been going through life, stuffing everything further down inside.

I would smile, and when I was asked what was wrong, I'd say "I'm fine."

The suffering inside screaming at me to reach out just this one time, denied.

No, I could handle this all on my own, labeled ultra-independent as I burdened myself,

Thinking I was strong going it alone, but really, I was too weak to simply ask for help.

. . .

Some think it is a weakness to ask for help, but there is strength in that kind of vulnerability,

A strength that I could not tap into for fear of being rejected, denied, or bullied.

Constantly told I feel too much, I'm too sensitive, or perhaps naive, craving to see positivity,

I kept trying to various altered states of me, convinced I'd fit their mold.....Eventually.

But I was not here to fit their mold, I was not here to simply sit down and conform,

I am the Phoenix, dark, light, or in-between, and from my ashes I am transformed.

The Phoenix tethered to me, part of me, burned the pain, the trauma, the past away,

She swept through my soul, my heart, and my mind to clear the path and show me the way.

What was left, just ashes of my past, ashes of my trauma, ashes of the pain and shame,

Burned to nothing as I stepped forward filled with light walking into a brighter better day.

The ashes around my feet swirling, some still sparkling as they reached the water of the lake,

The moon shining brightly behind me, as I step forward on my new path wide awake.

The Phoenix, there ever present, she will never forsake me or abandon me, I've only to ask,

To ask her for help, to bare my soul, to be vulnerable to her, to show up completely unmasked.

So, perhaps, she and I would burn the city to the ground to cleanse it of its depravity.

To prevent those that visited evils upon us, to cleanse the city of immorality and brutality.

Perhaps we too would scream as we allowed ourselves to feel everything all at once.

And disperse all the trauma, the hatred, the abuse, that was ever visited upon us.

It is possible and yet, we did burn it all down, we just did it in our mind privately,

Giving ourselves the freedom to move forward with purpose, healing, and love defiantly.

Now we know we can burn it all to ashes if ever the time should call for it again,

And we will always rise from those ashes stronger, our fire burning even more intense.

About the Author

Michol Mae is the founder of Lady Mae Impressions, and a talented artist, best-selling author, educator, poet, and musician. She intuitively weaves her wisdom, experiences, practice, and knowledge of creative writing, meditation, shamanism, and sound and energy healing into her programs, poetry, music, and novels as a way to combat abuse, trauma, grief, and to help others feel less alone on their journey. She is on a mission to grow emotional intelligence and normalize discussing mental health. Michol loves all furry friends, and you'll find her cats, Mac Lir and Cheeky Neeky, on her social media. Connect with Michol on her website: https://www.ladymaeimpressions.com